First World War
and Army of Occupation
War Diary
France, Belgium and Germany

2 DIVISION
Headquarters, Branches and Services
General Staff
1 October 1918 - 31 October 1918

WO95/1303

The Naval & Military Press Ltd
www.nmarchive.com
Published in association with The National Archives

Published by

The Naval & Military Press Ltd

Unit 10 Ridgewood Industrial Park,
Uckfield, East Sussex,
TN22 5QE England
Tel: +44 (0) 1825 749494

www.naval-military-press.com

www.nmarchive.com

This diary has been reprinted in facsimile from the original. Any imperfections are inevitably reproduced and the quality may fall short of modern type and cartographic standards.

© **Crown Copyright**
Images reproduced by permission of The National Archives, London, England, 2015.

Contents

Document type	Place/Title	Date From	Date To
Heading	B.E.F. France & Flanders. 2 Division H.Q. General Staff. 1918 Oct.		
Heading	2nd Division War Diaries General Staff October 1918		
War Diary	L. 13 C. 1.3 West of Flesquieres	01/10/1918	09/10/1918
War Diary	Flesquieres L.13 C.1.3 Move at 1000 to J.10 a. 3.1 N. of Doignies	09/10/1918	12/10/1918
War Diary	J. 10 a. 3.1 N. of Doignies	12/10/1918	12/10/1918
War Diary	Flesquieres J.10 a.3.1 Moved at 0930 to Chateau Seranvillers	13/10/1918	13/10/1918
Miscellaneous	Chateau Seranvillers	14/10/1918	21/10/1918
War Diary	Chateau Seranvillers Moved at 1000 to St Hilaire	22/10/1918	22/10/1918
War Diary	St Hilaire	23/10/1918	23/10/1918
War Diary	St Hilaire move at 0600 to St Python D. 6 a. 7.2	24/10/1918	24/10/1918
War Diary	St Pyton. D.6.a.7.2.	24/10/1918	31/10/1918
Heading	2nd Division War Diaries General Staff October 1918		
Miscellaneous	A Form Messages And Signals.		
Miscellaneous	Narrative of Operations 2nd Division.	09/10/1918	09/10/1918
Miscellaneous	Account Of Operations 8th October. 1918.	08/10/1918	08/10/1918
Miscellaneous	2nd Division "G"	12/10/1918	12/10/1918
Miscellaneous	October 1st-2nd.		
Miscellaneous	Report On Operations From 23rd. September To 4th October 1918		
Miscellaneous	Remarks and Suggestions arising From the Actions 27th September 3rd October 1918		
Map	France		
Miscellaneous	To accompany S.T. 6624		
Miscellaneous	Report On Operations From 27th September 1918	27/09/1918	27/09/1918
Miscellaneous	2nd Divisional Artillery Instructions No 1	03/10/1918	03/10/1918
Miscellaneous	2nd Divisional Artillery Instructions No 2	05/10/1918	05/10/1918
Miscellaneous	2nd Divisional Artillery Instructions No 3 Warning Order	06/10/1918	06/10/1918
Miscellaneous	Report On Operations from 5th to 9th October 1918 (Inclusive)	09/10/1918	09/10/1918
Miscellaneous	Summary of Operations for period 1st-9th October 1918 2nd Signal Coy. R.E.	09/10/1918	09/10/1918
Diagram etc	Diagram of Communications 2nd Division Night of Oct Xth 1918		
Map	Map Showing Lines-2nd Division-Night Oct 8th 1918		
Miscellaneous	57 C NE		
Miscellaneous	A Form. Messages And Signals. Appendix II		
Miscellaneous	A Form Messages And Signals. Appendix III		
Miscellaneous	A Form Messages And Signals. Appendix IV		
Miscellaneous	A Form. Messages And Signals. Appendix V		
Miscellaneous	A Form. Messages And Signals. Appendix VI		
Miscellaneous	A Form Messages And Signals Appendix VIII		
Miscellaneous	A Form. Messages And Signals.		
Miscellaneous	Appendix XIV		
Miscellaneous	Messages And Signals.		
Miscellaneous	2nd Division. Appendix XV		
Miscellaneous	Appendix XVI		

Type	Description	Date	Date
Miscellaneous	A Form. Messages And Signals.		
Miscellaneous			
Operation(al) Order(s)	2nd Division Order No. 361	06/10/1918	06/10/1918
Map	German Trenches in Blue.		
Miscellaneous	Distribution		
Miscellaneous	2nd Division Instructions No 1 (to accompany 2nd Division Order No. 361) Appendix XX	06/10/1918	06/10/1918
Map	To Accompany Instructions No 1		
Miscellaneous	A Form. Messages And Signals. Appendix XXII		
Operation(al) Order(s)	2nd Division Order No. 362	07/10/1918	07/10/1918
Miscellaneous	Addendum No. 1 To 2nd Division Order No. 361 Appendix XXIV	07/10/1917	07/10/1917
Miscellaneous	Locations 2nd Division Appendix XXV		
Map	Our Men Seen Enemy Seen Time		
Miscellaneous	Appendix XXVI A		
Map	Our Men Seen Enemy Seen Time		
Miscellaneous	Appendix XXVI A		
Map	Appendix XXVI B		
Miscellaneous	Message Form		
Miscellaneous	A Form Messages And Signals. Appendix XXVI		
Map	Appendix XXVI C		
Miscellaneous	Appendix XXVI C		
Miscellaneous	A Form Messages And Signals. Appendix XXVII		
Miscellaneous	A Form Messages And Signals. Appendix XXVIII		
Miscellaneous	A Form Messages And Signals. Appendix XXIX		
Map	Appendix XXX		
Miscellaneous	Message Form Appendix XXX		
Miscellaneous	A Form. Messages And Signals Appendix XXXI		
Miscellaneous	A Form Messages And Signals. Appendix XXXII		
Miscellaneous	A Form Messages And Signals Appendix XXXIII		
Miscellaneous	A Form Messages And Signals Appendix XXXIV		
Miscellaneous	A Form Messages And Signals Appendix XXXV		
Map	Dispositions of 2nd Div 9th Oct-1918		
Miscellaneous	Appendix XXXVI		
Miscellaneous	A Form Messages And Signals Appendix XXXVII		
Miscellaneous	A Form Messages And Signals Appendix XXXVIII		
Miscellaneous	Locations 2nd Division Appendix XXXIX	09/10/1918	09/10/1918
Miscellaneous	Locations 2nd Division 11th October 1918 Appendix XL	11/10/1918	11/10/1918
Miscellaneous	2nd Division No G.S. 948/17 Appendix XL (A)	11/10/1918	11/10/1918
Miscellaneous	2nd Division No. G.S. 948/17/1 Appendix XL (B)	13/10/1918	13/10/1918
Operation(al) Order(s)	2nd Division Order No. 363 Appendix XLI	12/10/1918	12/10/1918
Miscellaneous	March Table To Accompany 2nd Division Order No. 363		
Miscellaneous	2nd Corps Division Appendix XLII	12/10/1918	12/10/1918
Miscellaneous	Changes In Nominal Rolls Of Officers. (I.e., Explantion of Increases And Decreases.)		
Miscellaneous	Locations 2nd Division 14 October 1918 Appendix XLIII	14/10/1918	14/10/1918
Miscellaneous	Locations 2nd Division 15th October 1918 Appendix XLIV	15/10/1918	15/10/1918
Miscellaneous	A Form Messages And Signals Appendix XLV		
Miscellaneous	Form Messages And Signals. Appendix XLVI		
Operation(al) Order(s)	2nd Division Order No. 364	19/10/1918	19/10/1918
Miscellaneous	Priority To 10th D.C.L.I. & Train. Appendix XLVIII		
Miscellaneous	A Form Messages And Signals Appendix XLIX		

Miscellaneous	Locations 2nd Division 20th October 1918 Appendix L	20/10/1918	20/10/1918
Miscellaneous	Changes In Nominal Rolls Of Officers. (I.e., Explantion of Increases And Decreases.)		
Miscellaneous	2nd Corps Division Appendix LA	19/10/1918	19/10/1918
Miscellaneous	Appendix LI		
Miscellaneous	A Form Messages And Signals Appendix LII		
Miscellaneous	A Form Messages And Signals Appendix LII A		
Miscellaneous	Locations 2nd Division Appendix LIII	21/10/1918	21/10/1918
Miscellaneous	A Form Messages And Signals Appendix LIV		
Miscellaneous	A Form Messages And Signals Appendix LV		
Miscellaneous	A Form Messages And Signals		
Operation(al) Order(s)	2nd Division Order No. 365 Appendix LVI	21/10/1918	21/10/1918
Map	Trenches revised from information received to 12-10-18		
Heading	2nd Division War Diaries General Staff October 1918		
Miscellaneous	Locations 2nd Division 22nd October 1918 Appendix LVII	22/10/1918	22/10/1918
Miscellaneous	A Form Messages And Signals Appendix LVIII		
Miscellaneous	Addendum No. 1 To 2nd Division Order No. 365 Appendix LIX	22/10/1918	22/10/1918
Miscellaneous	Locations 2nd Division Appendix LX	23/10/1918	23/10/1918
Miscellaneous	A Form Messages And Signals Appendix LXI		
Operation(al) Order(s)	2nd Division Order No. 366 Appendix LXII		
Miscellaneous	A Form Messages And Signals Appendix LXIII		
Miscellaneous	A Form Messages And Signals Appendix LXIV		
Miscellaneous	A Form Messages And Signals Appendix LXV		
Miscellaneous	A Form Messages And Signals Appendix LXVI		
Miscellaneous	A Form Messages And Signals Appendix LXIX		
Miscellaneous	A Form Messages And Signals Appendix LXX		
Miscellaneous	A Form Messages And Signals Appendix LXXI		
Miscellaneous	Locations 2nd Division Appendix LXXII	24/10/1918	24/10/1918
Miscellaneous	A Form Messages And Signals Appendix LXXIII		
Miscellaneous	A Form Messages And Signals Appendix LXXIV		
Miscellaneous	A Form Messages And Signals		
Miscellaneous	A Form Messages And Signals Appendix LXXV		
Miscellaneous	Messages And Signals Appendix LXXVI		
Miscellaneous	A Form Messages And Signals Appendix LXXVII		
Miscellaneous	A Form Messages And Signals Appendix LXXVIII		
Miscellaneous	A Form Messages And Signals Appendix LXXIX		
Miscellaneous	Locations 2nd Division Appendix LXXX	25/10/1918	25/10/1918
Miscellaneous	A Form Messages And Signals Appendix LXXXI		
Miscellaneous	A Form Messages And Signals Appendix LXXXII		
Miscellaneous	A Form Messages And Signals		
Miscellaneous	Urgent Operations Priority to Appendix LXXXIII		
Miscellaneous	Locations 2nd Division Appendix LXXXIV	26/10/1918	26/10/1918
Miscellaneous	Locations 2nd Division Appendix LXXXV	27/10/1918	27/10/1918
Miscellaneous	2nd Corps Division Appendix LXXXVI	26/10/1918	26/10/1918
Miscellaneous	Changes In Nominal Rolls Of Officers. (I.e., Explantion of Increases And Decreases.)		
Miscellaneous	Explanation of Increase and Decrease		
Miscellaneous	Explanation of Column "B"		
Miscellaneous	A Form Messages And Signals Appendix LXXXVII		
Miscellaneous	A Form Messages And Signals Appendix LXXXVIII		
Miscellaneous	A Form Messages And Signals Appendix LXXXIX		
Miscellaneous	A Form Messages And Signals Appendix XC		
Miscellaneous	2nd Division No. G.U. 4/11 Appendix XCI	27/10/1918	27/10/1918
Miscellaneous	A Form Messages And Signals Appendix XCII		

Miscellaneous	Locations 2nd Division Appendix XCIII	29/10/1918	29/10/1918
Miscellaneous	A Form Messages And Signals Appendix XCIV		
Miscellaneous	A Form Messages And Signals Appendix XCV		
Miscellaneous	A Form Messages And Signals Appendix XCVI		
Miscellaneous	A Form Messages And Signals Appendix XCVII		
Operation(al) Order(s)	2nd Division Order No. 367 Appendix XCVIII	29/10/1918	29/10/1918
Miscellaneous	2nd Division No G.R 4/2	29/10/1918	29/10/1918
Miscellaneous	2nd Division No. G.R. 4/3 Appendix XCVIII a	29/10/1918	29/10/1918
Miscellaneous	Instructions referred to para. 3 2nd Division Order 367	29/10/1918	29/10/1918
Map	German Trenches in Blue.		
Map			
Miscellaneous	Main		
Miscellaneous	Report On Operations from 27th September 2nd Signal Co. R.E.	06/10/1918	06/10/1918
Miscellaneous	Locations 2nd Division Appendix CIV	01/11/1918	01/11/1918
Operation(al) Order(s)	2nd Division Warning Order No. 368 Appendix CIII	31/10/1918	31/10/1918
Miscellaneous	2nd Division No. G.R. 4/9 Appendix CII	31/10/1918	31/10/1918
Miscellaneous	Locations 2nd Division Appendix CI	31/10/1918	31/10/1918
Miscellaneous	2nd Division No. G.R. 4/7 Appendix C	30/10/1918	30/10/1918
Miscellaneous	Locations 2nd Division Appendix XCIX	30/10/1918	30/10/1918
Miscellaneous	2nd Division No. G.S. 1749	04/10/1918	04/10/1918
Miscellaneous	Changes In Nominal Rolls Of Officers. (I.e., Explantion of Increases And Decreases.)		
Miscellaneous	Other Ranks		
Miscellaneous	Explanation of Column "B"		
Miscellaneous	Explanation of Increase and Decrease		
Map	France		
Miscellaneous			
Miscellaneous	2nd Division No. GR. 5/1	30/10/1918	30/10/1918
Miscellaneous	2nd Division No. G.R. 4/6	30/10/1918	30/10/1918
Miscellaneous	2nd Division No. G.R. 4/10		
Map	France		
Map			
Miscellaneous	Preliminary		
Map	Map of Proposed Signal Communications		
Miscellaneous			

B.E.F. FRANCE & FLANDERS.

2 DIVISION

H.Q. GENERAL STAFF.

1918 OCT.

B.E.F. FRANCE & FLANDERS

2 DIVISION

H.Q. GENERAL STAFF.

1918 OCT.

1303

2nd Division

War Diaries

General Staff

October 1918

Dec

Army Form C. 2118.

WAR DIARY
or
INTELLIGENCE SUMMARY.
(Erase heading not required.)

Instructions regarding War Diaries and Intelligence Summaries are contained in F. S. Regs., Part II. and the Staff Manual respectively. Title pages will be prepared in manuscript.

Place	Date	Hour	Summary of Events and Information	Remarks and references to Appendices
L.13.c.1.3. West of FLESQUIERES.	Oct.1st.		Night 30th.Sept./1st.Oct. passed quietly. Command of Div. Sector in front line passed from G.O.C. 99th. Bde to G.O.C. 5th. Bde at 0100.	
		0600	Zero hour. Attack by 5th. Bde began. Considerable opposition still encountered and our troops were again held up by heavy M.G. fire from MONT SUR L'OEUVRE but succeeded in making some progress. The 3rd. Division attacked RUMILLY (in conjunction with 2nd. Division) on the right and made some progress but did not succeed in clearing the enemy out of RUMILLY.	
		0810	52nd. Light Infantry report 0730 troops on right advancing, left Company held up. British troops seen in RUMILLY and enemy shelling the village.	
		1015	Aeroplane message from 3rd. Division reported our troops were meeting with stubborn resistance on MASNIERES - CAMBRAI road and also in trenches in G.9.b. & c. Our troops now in shell holes in G.14.b & d. and also in trenches in G.14.d. and G.8.b & d. Several reports received from F.O.Os. and Observers during the morning stated our men were advancing over ridge in G.6.12.18 and 24 towards SERANVILLERS & NIERGNIES. These reports however were not confirmed by 5th. Bde, and appear to have been parties of the enemy going back. The situation being somewhat obscure and our men held up by M.G. fire from MONT SUR L'OEUVRE and RUMILLY which was still not cleared of the enemy, it was decided to renew the attack at 1830 in conjunction with 3rd. Division on our right.	App. 1.
		1720	2nd. Division G.207 issued (Appendix 1) orders for attack by 5th. Bde at 1830.	
		1830	Zero hour. Attack by 5th. Bde in conjunction with 3rd. Division began, and progressed satisfactorily.	
		1943	5th. Bde report capture of houses at G.9.a.7.9. at 1920 with 6 prisoners.	
		2005	5th. Bde report 24th. R. Fusiliers going well across MASNIERES - CAMBRAI road. 2nd.H.L.I. established on road, and working down trench S.E. from G.9.a.7.9. to railway. Enemy retaliation fairly heavy.	
		2055	VI Corps G.38 received (Appendix 11) orders for 2nd. October.	App.11.

Army Form C. 2118.

WAR DIARY
or
INTELLIGENCE SUMMARY.
(Erase heading not required.)

Instructions regarding War Diaries and Intelligence Summaries are contained in F.S. Regs., Part II. and the Staff Manual respectively. Title pages will be prepared in manuscript.

Place	Date	Hour	Summary of Events and Information	Remarks and references to Appendices
L.13.c.1.3. West of FLESQUIERES.	Oct.1st.contd.	2235.	2nd. Division G.219 issued (Appendix 111) orders to 5th. Bde for 2nd. October.	App.111.
	Oct.2nd.	0025	3rd. Division report RUMILLY captured. Owing to the failure of 52nd. Division on our left to capture the redoubt in A.27.a., and the FAUBERG de PARIS further advance by 5th. Bde was held up owing to heavy M.G. fire encountered from these places. 3rd. Division on our right made slight progress during the day, and established themselves along trench running through G.16 & 23.	
		0110	5th. Bde reported their dispositions as follows :- 24th. R. Fusiliers on right holding road from G.9.d.5.2. - G.9.b.8.0. thence N.W. along trench to railway. 2nd. H.L.I. on the left in touch with 24th. R. Fusiliers at junction of trench and railway at G.9.b.5.5. thence G.3.d.5.0. - G.3.c.9.5. - G.3.a. central - A.27.c.8.0. 52nd. L.I. in support in G.1.d. and G.8.d.	
		1540	B.G.G.S. VI Corps told G.S.O.1 on telephone that as a result of successful operations on Fourth Army front the Cavalry Corps might get through, in which case the VI Corps would attack the SERANVILLERS Ridge. This attack would be carried out by the 3rd. Division and the 2nd. Division would form a defensive flank North of 3rd. Division. No further engagements took place during the day. The 5th. Bde established an observation post in G.15.d. during the afternoon.	
		1840	2nd. Division G.244 issued (Appendix IV) orders for posts to be established by 5th. Bde.	App.IV.
		1925	VI Corps G.58 received (Appendix V) 1 Field Coy R.E. to be placed at disposal of C.E. VI Corps.	App.V.
		1940	VI Corps G.57 received (Appendix VI) orders for 3rd. October. Nothing further of importance took place during the day. The night 2nd/3rd. October passed quietly.	App.VI

Army Form C. 2118.

WAR DIARY
or
INTELLIGENCE SUMMARY
(Erase heading not required.)

Instructions regarding War Diaries and Intelligence Summaries are contained in F.S. Regs, Part II. and the Staff Manual respectively. Title pages will be prepared in manuscript.

Place	Date	Hour	Summary of Events and Information	Remarks and references to Appendices
L.13.c.1.3. West of FLESQUIERES.	Oct.3rd.	0555	52nd. Division on our left reported the capture of redoubt in A.27.a.	
		1015	Orders were issued for 6th. Bde to relieve 5th. Bde during the night 3rd/4th. October. See 2nd. Division G.258. (Appendix VII).	App.VII.
		1240	5th. Bde reported they were in touch with 3rd. Division at G.16.a.4.7.	
		1250	VI Corps telephoned to G.S.O.1 that operations on the Fourth Army front had been very successful, and that it was possible that the Cavalry Corps might go through between 1200 and 1400. This might affect the VI Corps front, and give an opportunity for carrying out the orders as given in VI Corps G.57 (See Appendix VI above). The enemy might possibly only hold the ground with M.Gs. which should not be regarded as an obstacle to our advance. There were 8 fighting tanks in Corps reserve which the Corps Commander intended to use if necessary, or if we wanted any special points dealt with, we could ask for some. The Tanks were either across the CANAL de ST QUENTIN or could cross at any time as tank bridges were ready and intact.	
		1435	5th. Bde were ordered to establish posts at G.11.c.0.0., G.10. central, G.10.d.5.4. and along the line G.3. central - G.11.c.3.1. See 2nd. Division G.263. (Appendix VIII).	App.VIII.
		1700	A warning order was issued to all units regarding the action to be taken by the 2nd. Division in conjunction with an attack by the 3rd. Division on SERANVILLERS in the event of the Cavalry getting through on the Fourth Army front and meeting with success. (See 2nd. Division G.267. Appendix IX)	App.IX.
		1835	As a result of telephone message from VI Corps all units were notified that the operation referred to above would not take place for 24 hours. See 2nd. Division G.270 (Appendix X)	App.X.
		2035	VI Corps G.88 received (See Appendix XI) orders for operations on 4th. October.	App.XI.
		2315	Relief of 5th. Bde by 6th. Bde complete. Command of 2nd. Division front passed to G.O.C. 6th. Bde. No engagements took place during the night 3/4th. October which passed quietly.	

Army Form C. 2118.

WAR DIARY
or
INTELLIGENCE SUMMARY.
(Erase heading not required.)

Instructions regarding War Diaries and Intelligence Summaries are contained in F.S. Regs., Part II. and the Staff Manual respectively. Title pages will be prepared in manuscript.

Place	Date	Hour	Summary of Events and Information	Remarks and references to Appendices
L.13.c.1.3. West of FLESQUIERES.	4th. Oct.	2020	The situation remained unchanged throughout the day, no infantry engagements took place. VI Corps G.108 received (See Appendix XII) cancelling operations ordered in VI Corps G.S.80/105 issued to Div. Commanders for the present. These orders outlined the operations which would take place in the event of the Cavalry breaking through on Fourth Army front. No change in the situation during the night 4/5th. October which passed quietly. Additional posts were established by the 6th. Bde as follows:- by 1st. Kings Regt at G.10.d.3.7., G.10.d.5.3., G.10.d.8.9., by 2nd. S. Staffs Regt. at G.4.c.4.4.	App. XII.
	5th. Oct.	0430 to 0500	NOYELLES lightly shelled with BLUE CROSS gas. During the morning Brig. Gen. W.L. OSBORN., C.M.G., D.S.O. Commanding 5th. Inf. Bde. was slightly wounded whilst visiting the 24th. R. Fusiliers in NOYELLES.	N/h. XIII
		1345	Notification was received from VI Corps that patrols of the IV & V Corps had crossed the CANAL de ST QUENTIN on the whole front. 2nd. & 3rd. Divisions were ordered to take advantage of any signs of withdrawal on the part of the enemy. (See VI Corps G.119. Appendix XIII). The left Battalion (2nd. S. Staffs. Regt.) established posts at G.3.b.4.5. and G.3.b.4.0. during the afternoon.	
		1930	B.G.G.S. VI Corps informed G.S.O.1 by telephone that the attack would be renewed on Monday 7th. October. No infantry engagements took place during the day. Hostile Artillery was intermittently active on our back areas.	
		2320	Orders received from VI Corps for 34th. A. Bde R.F.A. and 95th. Bde R.F.A. to move to 38th. & 21st. Divisions respectively forthwith. See VI Corps order H.190. Appendix XIV.	App. XIV.
		2430	VI Corps H.191 received.(Appendix XV) ordering transfer of 74th. Bde R.F.A. to XVII Corps. 2nd. Division Strength Return issued. Appendix XVa. Winter time came into force at midnight 5/6th. October when clocks were put back 1 hour. Posts were established by the right Battalion (1st. Kings. Regt.) at G.10.a.4.3., G.10.a.2.4., and G.10.a.2.5. during the night.	App. XV. App. XVa.

Army Form C. 2118.

WAR DIARY
or
~~INTELLIGENCE SUMMARY.~~
(Erase heading not required.)

Instructions regarding War Diaries and Intelligence Summaries are contained in F. S. Regs., Part II. and the Staff Manual respectively. Title pages will be prepared in manuscript.

Place	Date	Hour	Summary of Events and Information	Remarks and references to Appendices
L.13.c.1.3. West of FLESQUIERES	6th. Oct.	0035.	Some heavy but erratic hostile shelling took place on left Battalion front between 0100 and 0400, otherwise the night 5/6th. October passed quietly.	
		0835.	VI Corps order No.387 received, orders for attack on 7th. October.	
		0915	VI Corps artillery instructions No.80 received. Artillery orders issued in conjunction with VI Corps order No.387.	
		0945	Conference at 2nd. Divn. Hd.Qrs. to arrange details and plans for attack on 7th. October. The following attended, G.O.C.; and G.S.O.1 2nd. Division. G.O.C. and G.S.O.1 63rd. Division. C.R.A. 2nd. Division. G.O.C. 99th. Inf. Bde.	
		0955	G.O.C. 2nd. Division and G.O.C. 63rd. Division attended conference at 3rd. Division Hd.Qrs. to arrange details for attack on 7th. October.	
		1330	Telephone message from XVII Corps saying operations had been postponed for 24 hours. C.R.A. and 99th. Bde informed.	
			VI Corps G.139 received postponing operations ordered in order G.387 for 24 hours. See Appendix XVI.	App.XVI.
		1525	Wire received from VI Corps saying in view of a rumour that the Central Powers had asked for an Armistice the enemy might attempt to fraternise with our troops under cover of a White Flag. No notice to be taken of this except as laid down in F.S.R. part 1. Chap.5. Section 85. See VI Corps G.140. Appendix XVII.	App.XVII.
		1920	Orders issued to C.R.E. to mark out track to be used by 99th. Bde as a route to their forming up position prior to the attack. See 2nd. Division G.321. Appendix XVIII.	App.XVIII
		2200	2nd. Division order No.361 issued (Appendix XIX) orders for the attack by 99th. Bde on 8th. October. 2nd. Division instructions No.1 issued (Appendix XX.) No infantry engagements took place during the day which passed quietly on the Division front. Occasional hostile shelling of our forward areas was carried out *at intervals*	App.XIX & XX.

Army Form C. 2118.

WAR DIARY
or
INTELLIGENCE SUMMARY.
(Erase heading not required.)

Instructions regarding War Diaries and Intelligence Summaries are contained in F.S. Regs., Part II. and the Staff Manual respectively. Title pages will be prepared in manuscript.

Place	Date	Hour	Summary of Events and Information	Remarks and references to Appendices
L.13.c.1.3. West of FLESQUIERES	Oct 6th contd.		at intervals throughout the day. Night of 6/7th October passed quietly.	
	Oct 7th.	1000	A patrol report from 1st. Kings Regt. received, giving details of enemy trench system in G.11.c. 99th Bde. and 63rd Division notified. See Appendix XXI.	App. XXI.
		1040	All units notified that ZERO hour would be at 0430 on 8th October. See 2nd Division G.338 Appendix XXII.	App. XXII
		1130	Orders issued to units for the withdrawal of 2nd Division to the ORIVAL WOOD - DEMICOURT Area, on relief by the Guards Division. See 2nd Div. Order No.362. Appendix XXIII.	App. XXIII.
		1300	Orders issued to units giving the forming up place, route thereto and line of opening barrage for the attack on 8th October. See Addendum No.1 to 2nd Div. Order 361. App. XXIV. No events of importance took place during the day. which passed quietly. 2nd Div. Locations Appendix XXV.	App. XXIV. App. XXV.
		2300	Units of 99th Bde. began to cross the River L'ESCAUT and the CANAL de ST QUENTIN on their way to their forming up positions for the attack. All three Battalions crossed the river and canal without incident, the bridges being clear of traffic and no hostile artillery fire was directed against the bridges.	
	Oct 8th.	0115	1st R. Berks Regt., rear Battalion of 99th Bde. completed crossing river L'ESCAUT and CANAL de ST QUENTIN.	
		0230	All Battalions of 99th Bde were formed up ready for the attack.	
		0430	ZERO hour. Attack by 99th Bde. in conjunction with 3rd Division on our right and 63rd Division on our left began.	
		0705	Aeroplane message and map timed 0630 dropped at Div. Headquarters, giving position of our troops in first objective at 0630. See map Appendix XXVI*a*. The attack was successful to begin with and the first objective gained without much difficulty. Troops for the second objective passed through the first objective at ZERO. *plus 150 minutes, & succeeded in forcing*	App. XXVI.

Army Form C. 2118.

WAR DIARY
or
INTELLIGENCE SUMMARY.
(Erase heading not required.)

Instructions regarding War Diaries and Intelligence Summaries are contained in F. S. Regs., Part II. and the Staff Manual respectively. Title pages will be prepared in manuscript.

Place	Date	Hour	Summary of Events and Information	Remarks and references to Appendices
L.13.c.1.3. West of FLESQUIERES	8th Oct contd.		plus 130 minutes and succeeded in gaining the line of the ESNES - CAMBRAI Road in H.1.d. and H.7.b.	
		0815	Enemy counter-attacked supported by Tanks, and our troops were forced back to the line of the first objective. Our troops again took up the offensive but made little progress.	
		0825	Map dropped by contact aeroplane showing position of our troops at 0820. See Map. Appendix XXVIb.	App. XXVIb.
		0845	Report received from the C.R.E. that the water in the CANAL de ST QUENTIN was falling slowly and had fallen 15 inches in the last 17 hours.	
		0850	G.O.C. 99th Bde rang up and said that the 1st. K.R.R.C. reported enemy tanks were attacking from direction of FORENVILLE. Our line was on the first objective. He asked that a protective barrage might be put down 400x East of first objective. C.R.A. informed and necessary arrangements made.	
		0920	G.O.C. 99th Bde rang up and said that a F.O.O. reported the enemy were counter-attacking through NIERGNIES with tanks, and that the 2nd and 63rd Divisions were back on their first objectives.	
		0925	C.R.E. reported water in CANAL de ST QUENTIN was still falling at the rate of 1 inch per hour. One pontoon bridge was out of action.	
		0930	G.S.O.1 telephoned to C.R.A. to put the heavy Artillery on to FORENVILLE and the railway in H.2 and H.9. This was done.	
		0947	G.O.C. 99th Bde rang up and asked for the protective barrage to be taken off the line 400x E. of first objective and put down again E. of 2nd objective, also for the heavies to be taken off FORENVILLE. C.R.A. informed.	
		0950	VI Corps rang up G.O.C. on telephone saying the Corps Commander considered it extremely important to capture FORENVILLE.	

WAR DIARY
or
INTELLIGENCE SUMMARY.

(Erase heading not required.)

Army Form C. 2118.

Place	Date	Hour	Summary of Events and Information	Remarks and references to Appendices
L.13.c.1.3. West of FLESQUIERES	8th Oct contd.	0950	Orders were issued to the 6th Bde to place one Battalion at the disposal of the 99th Bde See 2nd Division G.379. Appendix XXVI. G.O.C. informed G.O.C. 99th Bde on the telephone that he might use the Battalion of the 6th Bde attached to 99th Bde to take the second objective. G.O.C. 6th Bde placed 17th Bn Royal Fusiliers at disposal of 99th Bde.	App. XXVI
		0955	C.R.A. rang up to say the barrage was now as requested by 99th Bde and that the Heavies had been taken off FORENVILLE.	
		1045	G.O.C. 99th Bde rang up and said the 99th Bde was on its first objective, the enemy were holding the Cemetery in H.1.c. road in H.1.d. H.7.b. and H.8.c., and FORENVILLE. He was just going up to find out the exact situation and to make arrangements for a further attack on FORENVILLE.	
		1140	Aeroplane message and map dropped, showing position of our troops. See map. Appendix XXVIc	App. XXVIc
		1240	All pontoon bridges in 2nd Division area out of action owing to water in the CANAL de ST QUENTIN still falling. Only bridge in action was the Trestle Bridge C. (See map). It was subsequently discovered that the reason for the water in the canal falling, was that the C.R.E. of a Division further North had opened a lock gate to raise the water level in his Divisional area, and had been unable to close the lock gate afterwards.	
		1420	Orders were issued to the 99th Bde for the attack to be renewed at 1500. See 2nd Division G.387. Appendix XXVII. If the attack failed another attempt to take FORENVILLE was to be made in conjunction with an attack by the 3rd Division at 1800. The 17th R. Fusiliers to be used for this purpose.	App. XXVII
		1500	Attack by 99th Bde resumed under cover of an Artillery barrage. Heavy M.G. fire was again encountered from FORENVILLE and from both flanks, and little progress was made.	
		1520	VI Corps G.197 received (App.XXVIII) orders for 2nd Division to complete the capture of the GREEN objective. The attack at 1500 by 99th Bde. having failed, no further attempts to reach the second objective was made until 1800, when the 1ᵗʰ R. Fusiliers attacked in conjunction with the 3rd Div. on our right.	App. XXVIII

Army Form C. 2118.

WAR DIARY
or
INTELLIGENCE SUMMARY
(Erase heading not required.)

Instructions regarding War Diaries and Intelligence Summaries are contained in F.S. Regs., Part II. and the Staff Manual respectively. Title pages will be prepared in manuscript.

Place	Date	Hour	Summary of Events and Information	Remarks and references to Appendices
L.13.c.1.3 West of FLESQUIERES	8th Oct contd.		When the 17th R. Fusiliers attacked in conjunction with the 3rd Division on our right.	
		1538	Orders received from VI Corps for Troops of Oxford Hussars attached to 2nd Division to rejoin their Squadron on 9th October.	App.XXX
		1620	Contact aeroplane report of our line. See map Appendix XXX.	
		1721	Orders received from VI Corps for 2nd Division to move back to reserve area after relief by Guards Division. See VI Corps G.200 AppendixXXXI.	App.XXXI
		1800	Attack on FORENVILLE by 17th R. Fusiliers in conjunction with 3rd Division who were attacking the ESNES - CAMBRAI road on our right. This attack was successful and FORENVILLE was captured together with about 60 prisoners and 5 Field Guns.	
		1945	Permission received from VII Corps to withdraw troops of 2nd Division through whom XVII Corps had passed. See VI Corps G.217 Appendix XXXII.	App.XXXII
		2000	Orders received from VI Corps to withdraw troops of 99th Bde. to a line 300x West of LA TARGETTE - CAMBRAI road by 0500 9th October in order to get them out of the way of the opening barrage for an attack by the Guards Division. See VI Corps G.206 Appendix XXXIII	App.XXXIII
		2210	Units were informed of attack by Guards Division on 9th October and all troops ordered to be withdrawn in accordance with instructions stated above. 2nd Division to be considered as relieved when the Guards Division had passed through. See 2nd. Division G.405 Appendix XXXIV.	App.XXXIV
		2240	2nd Division G.406 issued (Appendix XXXV) orders for move of units on 9th October. Night 8/9th October passed quietly. In the early morning 1st K.R.R.C. pushed forward posts to within 300x of the ESNES - CAMBRAI road. Troops of 99th Bde. were withdrawn to a line 300x West of LA TARGETTE - CAMBRAI road during the night.	App.XXXV
	9th Oct.	0520	ZERO hour for attack by Guards Division, at which hour Guards Division passed through	

Army Form C. 2118.

WAR DIARY

~~INTELLIGENCE~~ ~~SUMMARY~~
(Erase heading not required.)

Instructions regarding War Diaries and Intelligence Summaries are contained in F. S. Regs., Part II. and the Staff Manual respectively. Title pages will be prepared in manuscript.

Place	Date	Hour	Summary of Events and Information	Remarks and references to Appendices
FLESQUIERES L.13.c.1.3. moved at 1000 to J.10.a.3.1. N. of DOIGNIES.	9th Oct.contd.		and relieved troops of 2nd Division on the whole of the Div. front. Command of Sector passed to G.O.C. Guards Division. Units of 2nd Division moved back to the following areas :- 5th Inf. Bde. to area between DEMICOURT and CANAL DU NORD, the Canal being exclusive to 5th Bde. 6th Inf. Bde. to area between CANAL DU NORD (inclusive) and the HINDENBURG SUPPORT line in K.10.b. & d. and K.16.b. 99th Inf Bde to FLESQUIERES - ORIVAL WOOD area. 10th D.C.L.I., 2nd M.G. Battalion to area between DEMICOURT and DOIGNIES. R.E. units were situated in the vicinity of the CANAL de ST QUENTIN about NOYELLES and MARCOING and employed on bridges over the river L'ESCAUT and the CANAL de ST QUENTIN. See map App. XXXVI.	App. XXXVI.
		1000	2nd Division Headquarters closed at L.13.c.1.3. and opened at DOIGNIES J.10.a.3.1.	
		1215	VI Corps H.198 received (see Appendix XXXVII) Artillery instructions giving allotment of H.A. & R.F.A. to Divisions. 9.2 Howitzers to be held in reserve.	App. XXXVII.
		2235	Orders were issued to the C.R.E. and 10th D.C.L.I. regarding work on and maintenance of bridges in the NOYELLES - MARCOING area. See 2nd Division G.16 Appendix XXXVIII. 2nd Division Locations Appendix XXXIX Units of 2nd Division spent the day organising and resting.	App. XXXVIII. App. XXXIX.
	10th Oct.		Units of 2nd Division carried out training and reorganised.	
	11th Oct.		Training continued. 2nd Division Locations Appendix XL.	App. XL.
	12th Oct.		Training continued. G.O.C. held a conference of Brigadiers, C.R.A. Artillery Bde. and Battalion Commanders at Headquarters of the 2nd S.Staffs Regt at 1400.	

WAR DIARY
or
INTELLIGENCE SUMMARY.
(Erase heading not required.)

Army Form C. 2118.

Place	Date	Hour	Summary of Events and Information	Remarks and references to Appendices
J.10.a.3.1. N. of DOIGNIES.	12th Oct. contd.		Tactics adopted during the recent operations and lessons learnt from them were discussed. See 2nd Div. G.S.948/17, points to be brought up at Div. conference, and 2nd Div. G.S.948/17/1 proceedings of Divn. conference. Appendices XL.a & b.	App. XL.a. XL.b.
		1930	Orders issued to units for the move of 2nd Div. to the SERANVILLERS area on 13th Oct. See 2nd Div. order No.363. Appendix XLl.	App. XLl.
			2nd Div. strength return issued. (Appendix XLll).	App. XLll.
FLESQUIERES J.10.a.3.1. moved at 0930 to CHATEAU SERANVILLERS	13th Oct.	0930	2nd Div. Headquarters closed at DOIGNIES J.10.a.3.1. and opened at the Chateau SERANVILLERS. Units of 2nd Div. marched to the following areas :- 5th Infantry Brigade. RUMILLY. 6th Infantry Brigade. NIERGNIES. 99th Infantry Brigade. WAMBAIX. 2nd M.G. Battalion. RUMILLY.	
			2nd Div. Locations (Appendix XLlll)	App.XLlll
		2130	VI Corps Order No.391 received, outline of orders issued by the Third Army to VI Corps. VI & XVII Corps to push forward to the LA SELLE River and to take any opportunity of establishing advanced Guards East of the river. Preparations to be made to attack the high ground East of the River SELLE on 17th Oct. in conjunction with V & IV Corps and the Fourth Army.	

Army Form C. 2118.

WAR DIARY
or
INTELLIGENCE SUMMARY.
(Erase heading not required.)

Instructions regarding War Diaries and Intelligence Summaries are contained in F. S. Regs., Part II. and the Staff Manual respectively. Title pages will be prepared in manuscript.

Place	Date	Hour	Summary of Events and Information	Remarks and references to Appendices
Chateau SERANVILLERS	14th Oct.		Training continued.	
			2nd Div. Locations. Appendix XLIV.	App. XLIV
		2115	Instructions received from VI Corps that it was not now intended to attack in conjunction with the Fourth Army on 17th October. Corps, however, had been ordered to be prepared to attack at short notice the high ground East of LA SELLE River on a date to be notified later, probably not before 20th October.	
	15th Oct.		No change in the situation.	
			Training continued by units of 2nd Div.	
	16th Oct.		Training continued.	
			No change in situation of 2nd Div.	
	17th Oct.		Training continued.	
			No change in situation of 2nd Div.	
	18th Oct.		Training continued.	
			No change in situation.	

Army Form C. 2118.

WAR DIARY
or
INTELLIGENCE SUMMARY.
(Erase heading not required.)

Instructions regarding War Diaries and Intelligence Summaries are contained in F.S. Regs., Part II. and the Staff Manual respectively. Title pages will be prepared in manuscript.

Place	Date	Hour	Summary of Events and Information	Remarks and references to Appendices
Chateau GRANVILLERS.	18th Oct. contd.	1420	As a result of verbal instructions received from VI Corps the 5th Bde. group was ordered to be prepared to move to the CARNIERES - BOUSSIERES area on 19th Oct. See 2nd Div. G.95. (Appendix XLV.)	AppXLV
		1545	VI Corps order 393 received. Orders for the resumption of attack by the Third Army objective LE QUESNOY. Guards and 62nd Divs. to carry out an attack on the night 19/20th Oct. with the object of securing the crossing over the River SELLE. 2nd and 3rd Divs. to be at 2 hours notice to move after 0700 20th Oct. 2nd Div. to move one brigade to the CARNIERES - BOUSSIERES area on 19th Oct.	
		1800	Orders issued to 5th Inf. Bde. group to move to the CARNIERES - BOUSSIERES area on 19th Oct. 5th Bde. Headquarters to take over Headquarters of 3rd Guards Bde. at CARNIERES. See 2nd Div. G.98. (Appendix XLVI).	AppXLVI
	19th Oct.	1015	Orders issued to units regarding the advance of the Third Army on LE QUESNOY. All troops of 2nd Div. ordered to be at 2 hours notice to move after 0700 20th Oct. (See 2nd Div. Order No.364. Appendix XLVII). Units of 5th Inf. Bde. Group moved from RUMILLY area to CARNIERES - BOUSSIERES area during the afternoon, move completed by 1935.	

Army Form C. 2118.

WAR DIARY
or
INTELLIGENCE SUMMARY.
(Erase heading not required.)

Place	Date	Hour	Summary of Events and Information	Remarks and references to Appendices
Chateau SERANVILLERS	19th Oct. contd.	1320	Orders received from VI Corps for Pioneer Battalion to move by 0900 on 20th Oct. to ST HILAIRE. 10th D.C.L.I. were accordingly ordered to move. See 2nd Div. G.113. (Appendix XLVIII.)	App. XLVIII
		1415.	Warning order received from VI Corps that the 2nd and 3rd Divs. were to be prepared to move forward to close billets on 20th Oct. 2nd Div. Bdes. to be located as follows :- "A" Bde. group ST HILAIRE. "B" " " BOUSSIERES & CARNIERES. "C" " " NIERGNIES. Div. Headquarters to remain at SERANVILLERS. At the same time 2nd & 3rd Divs. were warned to be prepared to pass through Guards & 62nd Divs. and to continue the advance on the early morning of 22nd October. Orders were issued by 2nd Div. to units in accordance with the above instructions. See 2nd Div. G.112. (Appendix XLIX).	App. XLIX.
		1518	Situation report from XVII Corps that enemy appear to be withdrawing on right of XXII Corps and on XVII Corps fronts. Orders for Guards and 62nd Divs. to push forward patrols and occupy high ground East of River SELLE should the enemy show signs of withdrawal on VI Corps front. A later situation report from VI Corps stated patrols of Guards and 62nd Divs. were fired at with rifles and M.Gs. during the afternoon. Hostile artillery normally active. 2nd Div. Locations. (Appendix L.)	App. L.

Army Form C. 2118.

WAR DIARY
or
INTELLIGENCE SUMMARY.
(Erase heading not required.)

Instructions regarding War Diaries and Intelligence Summaries are contained in F. S. Regs., Part II. and the Staff Manual respectively. Title pages will be prepared in manuscript.

Place	Date	Hour	Summary of Events and Information	Remarks and references to Appendices
Chateau SERANVILLERS	20th Oct.	0200	ZERO hour for attack by Guards and 62nd Divs. in conjunction with IV Corps on their right and XVII Corps on their left.	
		0718	Orders received from VI Corps for 2nd and 3rd Divisions to move forward in accordance with instructions contained in VI Corps warning order No.394 para.1. G.O.s.O. 2nd and 3rd Divs. to report at Corps Headquarters at 1000 morning of 20th Oct. See VI Corps G.155. Appendix LI.	App.LI.
		0745	Orders were received from VI Corps that owing to indications that the enemy might not accept battle on his present line, the Guards and 62nd Divs. were to be prepared to push forward advanced guards to the following line :- W.17.d.5.8. - W.11.c.0.0. - W.4.d.0.0. - Q.34.a.0.0. - Q.27.d.0.1. and to back up their advanced guards with their main bodies as soon as two Bdes of Field Artillery on each Div. sector had crossed the river SELLE, the final objective being the line R.W.31.d.5.0. - R.31.c.0.6. - Q.36.c.1.7. - Q.35.a.6.0. - Q.27.d.0.1. If, however, serious opposition was encountered touch was to be maintained with the enemy and no further attack made until 22nd Oct. when the 2nd and 3rd Divs. would go through the Guards and 62nd Divs. respectively to gain the objectives mentioned above.	
		0755	Orders issued to units to move forward in accordance with VI Corps warning order No.394. See 2nd Div. G.123. Appendix LII.	App.LII.
		1000	G.O.C. and G.S.O.1 attended conference at VI Corps Headquarters to discuss details for attack to be carried out on 22nd Oct. Later in the day this attack was postponed for 24 hours.	

Army Form C. 2118.

WAR DIARY
or
~~INTELLIGENCE SUMMARY~~

(Erase heading not required.)

Instructions regarding War Diaries and Intelligence Summaries are contained in F. S. Regs., Part II. and the Staff Manual respectively. Title pages will be prepared in manuscript.

Place	Date	Hour	Summary of Events and Information	Remarks and references to Appendices
Chateau SERANVILLERS	20th Oct. contd.		See VI Corps G.167. Appendix LII.a.	App.LIIa.
		1410	As result of orders received from VI Corps, G.131 was issued to C.R.E. and 10th. D.C.L.I. instructions regarding maintenance of the ST VAAST - ST PYTHON road to river SELLE.	App.LIV.
			See Appendix LIV.	
			No change in the situation of the 2nd Div. took place during the day.	
			2nd Div. Locations. Appendix LIII.	App.LIII.
	21st Oct.	1000	G.O.C. and G.S.O.I attended conference at VI Corps Headquarters. Plans for the attack on the 23rd Oct. were discussed and arrangements made to coordinate the attack with that of the Flank Corps.	
		1715	Orders for attack and Zero hour on 23rd Oct. received from VI Corps. Zero hour for VI Corps to be 0320 on 23rd Oct.	
		2325	Orders issued to units to move forward to the ST HILAIRE - ST VAAST - ST PYTHON area on 22nd Oct.	
			See 2nd Div. G.143. Appendix LV.	App.LV.
		2340	2nd Div. order No.385 and map issued-see Appendix LVI. Orders to units for the attack on 23rd Oct.	App.LVI.
			2nd Div. Locations. Appendix LVII.	App.LVII.

Army Form C. 2118.

WAR DIARY
or
INTELLIGENCE SUMMARY
(Erase heading not required.)

Instructions regarding War Diaries and Intelligence Summaries are contained in F. S. Regs., Part II. and the Staff Manual respectively. Title pages will be prepared in manuscript.

Place	Date	Hour	Summary of Events and Information	Remarks and references to Appendices
Chateau SERANVILLERS moved at 1000 to ST HILAIRE.	22nd Oct.	1000	Div. Headquarters closed at SERANVILLERS and opened at ST HILAIRE C.12.b.6.7.	
		1225.	5th Bde. C.R.A. and 2nd M.G. Battalion notified time of Zero hour for 23rd October. See 2nd Div. G.155. Appendix LVIII.	App.LVII
		1330	Addendum No.1 to 2nd Div. order No.365 issued. Alteration in line of opening barrage. 5th Inf. Bde. to relieve 1st and 3rd Guards Bdes. during night 22/23rd Oct. 2nd M.G. Batt. to relieve forward guns of Guards M.G. Battalion. See Appendix LIX.	App.LIX.
			The following moves took place during the day:- 5th Bde. from ST HILAIRE - ST VAAST area to ST PYTHON area. 99th Bde. from CARNIERES - BOUSSIERES area to ST HILAIRE area, with one Battalion (23rd R. Fusiliers) in ST PYTHON. 6th Bde. from NIERGNIES area to ST HILAIRE area.	
			5th Bde. relieved 1st and 3rd Guards Bdes. during the evening. Command of sector passed to G.O.C. 2nd Div. at 2145.	
			2nd Div. Locations. Appendix LX.	App.LX.
ST HILAIRE.	23rd Oct.		Considerable shelling of ST PYTHON area took place during the night 22/23rd Oct., otherwise nothing of importance took place.	
		0240	The 5th Inf. Bde. formed up ready for the attack without trouble. 23rd Bn. R. Fusiliers established East of River SELLE.	

WAR DIARY
or
~~INTELLIGENCE SUMMARY~~

Army Form C. 2118.

(*Erase heading not required.*)

Place	Date	Hour	Summary of Events and Information	Remarks and references to Appendices
ST HILAIRE.	23rd Oct. contd.	0320	Zero hour. 5th Bde in conjunction with the 3rd Div. on the right and the 19th Div. on the left attacked under cover of an Artillery barrage. The objectives being as shewn on map issued with 2nd Div. order No.365. See Appendix LVI. The attack was supported by 5th Bde. Field Artillery, consisting of the Guards and 2nd Divl. Artilleries and the 14th R.H.A. Bde.	
			The 24th Bn. R. Fusiliers attacked on the right and the 2nd Bn. H.L.I. on the left and succeeded in gaining the first objective without encountering much opposition from the enemy. The capture of first objective was completed by about 0510, our casualties were very light, 5 Officers and 217 O.R. prisoners were taken by us.	
			Touch was established and maintained with the Divns. on our flanks, both of which succeeded in gaining their objectives and took a considerable number of prisoners.	
		0840	Zero hour for 2nd (Green) objective.	
		1000	VI Corps G.S.80/271. Further orders for attack on 23rd October, received.	
		1025	As a result of instructions received from VI Corps, one troop of Oxford Hussars and detachment of Cyclists attached to 2nd Div. were ordered to proceed at once and report to Headquarters 3rd Div. at ST PYTHON.	
			See 2nd Div. G.9. (Appendix LXI.)	App.LXI
		1040	Report received from F.O.O. timed Q918 that our troops were advancing through ESCARMAIN with very little opposition, and had gained the N. and E. edge of village and were in touch with 3rd Div. on our right. 3rd Div. had reached sunken road in W.6.c.	

Army Form C. 2118.

WAR DIARY
or
INTELLIGENCE SUMMARY

(Erase heading not required.)

Place	Date	Hour	Summary of Events and Information	Remarks and references to Appendices
ST HILAIRE.	23rd Oct. contd.	1145	5th Bde. report that 2nd H.L.I. were established on second objective and were in touch with 57th Bde. on their left.	
		1200	2nd Div. order No.368 issued. See Appendix LXII. If the attack developes favourably Oxford Hussars and Cyclists will follow up the enemy, objective being to occupy RUESNES and high ground in its vicinity on night 23rd Oct. After capture of BROWN objective 5th Inf. Bde. to push forward patrols to River ECAILLON and occupy the river crossings. If Oxford Hussars occupy village of RUESNES, 5th Bde. to push forward not less than one Battalion to high ground in Q.24 with a second Battalion in support N. of the ECAILLON.	AppLXII
		1234	Orders received from VI Corps to move our support Bde. to neighbourhood of VERTAIN at once and reserve Bde. to neighbourhood of ST PYTHON on evening 23rd Oct. See VI Corps G.242. Appendix LXIII.	AppLXIII
		1310	Warning order received from VI Corps giving objectives for 24th October. The line R.15.d.0.0. - R.14 central - R.7 central to be captured as a main line of resistance. Mounted troops with infantry advanced guards to exploit success forward of this line. 2nd and 3rd Divns. to carry out this advance. Corps mounted troops directed on VILLERS - POL. See VI Corps G.241. (Appendix LXIV).	AppLXIV
		1355	2nd Div. G.14 issued. Orders to units for moves to take place on 23rd Oct. See Appendix LXV.	App.LXV.
		1425	Orders issued to 99th Bde. to move at once to VERTAIN area. See 2nd Div. G.18 Appendix LXVI.	App.LXVI.
		1430	Zero hour for attack on third objective (BROWN). Attack started well and progressed	

Army Form C. 2118.

WAR DIARY
or
INTELLIGENCE SUMMARY.
(Erase heading not required.)

Instructions regarding War Diaries and Intelligence Summaries are contained in F.S. Regs., Part II. and the Staff Manual respectively. Title pages will be prepared in manuscript.

Place	Date	Hour	Summary of Events and Information	Remarks and references to Appendices
ST HILAIRE.	23rd Oct. contd.		favourably, our troops reached their objective without much difficulty and pushed forward to the CAPELLE - BERMERAIN road, capturing CAPELLE with several prisoners. Patrols were pushed forward to the West side of the ECAILLON river, but were unable to cross the river owing to fairly heavy M.G. fire from the high ground to the North of it. The line mentioned above was consolidated and held as a main line of resistance.	
			No enemy counter attack took place.	
			Touch was established and maintained with the 3rd Div. on the right and the 19th Div. on the left.	
			No further engagements took place during the day.	
		1900	VI Corps orders received giving objectives for 24th Oct. Advance to be continued at 0400. Corps mounted troops directed on VILLERS - POL. See VI Corps G.250. Appendix LXVII	AppLXVII
		1900	Orders issued to units for attack on 24th Oct. 99th Bde. to relieve 5th Bde. during night 23/24th Oct. and to carry out the attack. See 2nd Div. G.29. Appendix LXVIII.	AppLXVIII
		1920	All concerned informed that Zero hour for attack on 24th Oct. would be 0400. See 2nd Div. G.30. Appendix LXIX.	AppLXIX
		2025	All concerned informed of line of opening barrage, and rate of advance for attack on 24th Oct. See 2nd Div. G.34. Appendix LXX.	App.LXX
		2030	99th Bde. ordered to push out patrols to high ground N. of railway in R.2 and 8. after reaching objective. All concerned informed. See 2nd Div. G.35. Appendix LXXI.	AppLXXI

WAR DIARY
~~INTELLIGENCE SUMMARY~~

(Erase heading not required.)

Army Form C. 2118.

Place	Date	Hour	Summary of Events and Information	Remarks and references to Appendices
ST HILAIRE.	23rd Oct. contd.		As a result of the days fighting 9 Officers and 434 O.R. prisoners had passed through Divn. Cage up to 1600. It is estimated that at least another 150 were captured. One Field Gun, 4 T.Ms. and several M.Gs. were also captured. The enemy in most cases appeared demoralised and surrendered readily. The 2nd Bn. H.L.I. alone actually counted 240 prisoners taken by them.	
			2nd Div. Locations. Appendix LXXII.	App LXXII
		2345	Relief of 5th Bde. by 99th Bde. complete. Command of sector passed to G.O.C. 99th Bde.	
ST HILAIRE. moved at 0600 to ST PYTHON D.6.a.7.2.	24th Oct.	0135	All units of 99th Bde. in position ready for attack at Zero.	
		0040	Zero hour. Attack by 99th Bde. in conjunction with 3rd Div. on the right and 61st. Div. on the left began. The attack was supported by 5 Bdes. of Field Artillery, the same Bdes. being employed as for the attack on 23rd Oct.	
			Attack on 2nd and 3rd Div. fronts progressed satisfactorily and the objective was gained without serious opposition being encountered. About 400 prisoners were taken by the 99th Bde. in this attack. Our casualties were light.	
		0630	2nd Div. Headquarters closed at ST HILAIRE and opened at ST PYTHON. D.6.a.7.2.	
		0800	6th Bde. were ordered to move at once to VERTAIN. See 2nd Div. G.46. Appendix LXIII.	App LXXIII
		1110	Orders received from VI Corps for 2nd and 3rd Divns. to drive the enemy East of the	

Army Form C. 2118.

WAR DIARY
or
~~INTELLIGENCE SUMMARY~~

(Erase heading not required.)

Instructions regarding War Diaries and Intelligence Summaries are contained in F.S. Regs., Part II. and the Staff Manual respectively. Title pages will be prepared in manuscript.

Place	Date	Hour	Summary of Events and Information	Remarks and references to Appendices
ST PYTHON. D.6.a.7.2.	24th Oct. contd.		LE QUESNOY - VALENCIENNES railway from R.16 central to R.1.d.5.0. General direction of advance to be VILLERS - POL - WARGNIES le GRAND. See VI Corps G.275. Appendix LXXIV.	AppLXXIV.
		1155	Orders received from VI Corps for Guards Div. Artillery to be withdrawn and revert to its own Div. as soon as 2nd Div. established on the line of resistance ordered in VI Corps G.250 of 23rd Oct. (See App. LXVII). See VI Corps H.L.212. Appendix LXXV.	AppLXXV.
		1220	Situation of 61st Div. notified to C.R.A. and 99th Bde. 99th Bde. ordered to consolidate main line of resistance and to hold line of the railway, including MORTRY FARM, with outposts. See 2nd Div. G.5. Appendix LXXVI.	AppLXXVI
		1300	Orders issued to 5th and 6th Bdes. to move Battalions as follows :- 5th Bde. 2 Battalions to ST PYTHON on afternoon 24th Oct. 6th Bde. 2 Battalions to ESCARMAIN. See 2nd Div. G.53. Appendix LXXVII.	AppLXXVII.
		1440	6th Bde. were ordered to place one Battalion at the disposal of 99th Bde. at once, to be used as reserve or to cover left flank of 99th Bde. See 2nd Div. G.54. Appendix LXXVIII.	AppLXXVIII.
		1800	As a result of a telephone order from 6th Corps, orders were issued to units that the line gained to-day was to be consolidated. Enemy to be harassed by all means available, and followed up vigorously if he showed signs of withdrawal. See 2nd Div.G.59. Appendix LXXIX.	AppLXXIX.
			No further fighting took place during the day.	

Army Form C. 2118.

WAR DIARY
or
INTELLIGENCE SUMMARY
(Erase heading not required.)

Instructions regarding War Diaries and Intelligence Summaries are contained in F.S. Regs., Part II. and the Staff Manual respectively. Title pages will be prepared in manuscript.

Place	Date	Hour	Summary of Events and Information	Remarks and references to Appendices
ST PYTHON. D.5.a.7.2.	24th Oct. contd.		Plans were considered for an attack on the LE QUESNOY - VALENCIENNES railway, but owing to the right flank of the 3rd Div. on our right being exposed to M.G. fire from LE QUESNOY this idea was given up. The 61st Div. on our left were hung up for some time just North of BERMERAIN owing to the situation on their left being somewhat obscure, and consequently a defensive flank had to be formed by the 99th Bde. from LA FOLIE FARM, where they were in touch with 61st Div., to cross roads in R.7.a. Later in the day the 61st Div. advanced their line to Q.12.d. and c, and Q.11.d.	
			2nd Div. Locations. Appendix. LXXX.	AppLXXX.
	25th Oct.		The night 24/25th Oct. passed quietly.	
			99th Bde. pushed out patrols towards the railway in R.1, R.7 and R.8, but these were held up by heavy M.G. fire from the Orchards in R.7.b. and R.8.a.	
			During the early morning the situation on the left Divn. front was cleared up, and at 0725 the 61st Div. reported that VENDEGIES was clear of the enemy and that their troops were East of the village. They also held the high ground in Q.11.a. and Q.12.c.	
		0615	Information from 3rd Div. on our right that a patrol report timed 0300 states railway line not held by enemy from R.9.d.3.0. - R.15.b. 5 prisoners captured by them in BELLE VUE FARM. Later patrol report timed 0430 states enemy hold railway with posts 200 yards S.W. of railway in R.15.b. M.G. fire and very lights from railway.	
		0745	Situation on 2nd Div. front as follows :- 99th Bde. report their line R.14.central to cross roads R.7.a.5.2. with left flank on tree Q.12.c.3.5. where in touch with 2/4th Oxford and Bucks. L.I. of 61st Div. Enemy holding railway line, also Orchards in R.8.a. with M.Gs.	

Army Form C. 2118.

WAR DIARY
or
INTELLIGENCE SUMMARY

(Erase heading not required.)

Instructions regarding War Diaries and Intelligence Summaries are contained in F. S. Regs., Part II. and the Staff Manual respectively. Title pages will be prepared in manuscript.

Place	Date	Hour	Summary of Events and Information	Remarks and references to Appendices
ST.PYTHON. D.6.a.7.2.	25th Oct. contd.	0757.	VI Corps telephoned that XVII Corps report from 61st Div. states one of their patrols had reached the railway south of SEPMERIES at 0700 and found it unoccupied. 99th Bde. were informed.	
		0905	61st Div. on our left report Patrols from right Battalion of right Bde. proceeded down road to Q.11.d.1.2. to railway and encountered no enemy.	
		0920	VI Corps telephoned that 3rd Div. reported they had occupied BELLE VUE FARM and found 30 civilians there who stated that enemy had retired in a N.E. direction. Patrols were being sent down to railway and if this information found to be correct, the 8th Bde. would be sent through to the line of the railway.	
		1005	61st Div. informed us by telephone that they were on the line of the railway from Q.6 to K.34, and were pushing patrols towards LA RHONELLE river, patrols were fired at from the high ground in K.29. and 30.	
		1130	Contact patrol report states no movement seen in line of pits in R.9.c. and R.15.a. & b. and no movement observed on roads.	
		1215	Bde. Major 99th Bde. rang up and said 1st R. Berks. were on the line of the railway and in touch with 61st Div. at R.1.c.9.4. at 1100.	
			Situation of 2nd Div. at 1215 as given by Brigadier 99th Bde. from our front line was that our troops were on the line of the railway on the whole Div. front. Patrols were pushing forward from the railway with apparently no opposition. Not in touch with 3rd Div. on the railway, but patrols of 24th R. Fusiliers were working along the railway to get it.	

WAR DIARY
INTELLIGENCE SUMMARY
(Erase heading not required.)

Army Form C. 2118.

Place	Date	Hour	Summary of Events and Information	Remarks and references to Appendices
ST-PYTHON. D.6.a.7.2.	25th Oct. contd.	1439	3rd Div. reported they held the line of the railway with patrols pushed forward in front.	
		1500	Report received from F.O.O. timed 1200, "Our men seen walking in Q.6.a. and c. No.M.G. or rifle fire near railway. Enemy shelling road R.7 central to RUESNES. 77 mm 5.9 How. and 4.2 How. also registering German Trig. Point on ridge B.7.c.0.5. At 1350 sharp concentration of 77 mm on line RUESNES - LE QUESNOY. All fire appears to come from L.15, L.36 and JENLAIN. Enemy could be seen occupying high ground from L.26.a.5.9. - L.27.b.9.8. Mounted men were riding up and down, evidently posting picquets. These were reported by LOVATS SCOUTS to be German Cavalry. One or two men seen carrying Machine Guns.	
		1510	Situation of 2nd Div. unchanged except that patrols of leading Battalions had reached the line of hedge in R.2.c.	
		1654	VI Corps K.213 received, ordering Guards and 62nd Divn Artilleries to revert to their own Divisions for rest and refit. See Appendix LXXXI.	App LXXXI
		1800	Orders received from VI Corps for 3rd Div. to take over the duties of advanced guard on whole Corps front at daylight 26th Oct. and passing through troops of 2nd Div. 2nd Div. to be responsible for the organisation and defence of Corps main line of resistance. See VI Corps order G.308. Appendix LXXXII.	App LXXXII
		1805	3rd Div. report their situation as follows :- holding line of the railway with Cavalry at LA CROISETTE. Party of enemy still at about R.16 central, but being dealt with by 3rd and N.Z Divisions.	
		1835	VI Corps telephoned that right Battalion of 61st Div. was in L.32.a. with one	

Army Form C. 2118.

WAR DIARY
or
INTELLIGENCE SUMMARY
(Erase heading not required.)

Instructions regarding War Diaries and Intelligence Summaries are contained in F. S. Regs., Part II. and the Staff Manual respectively. Title pages will be prepared in manuscript.

Place	Date	Hour	Summary of Events and Information	Remarks and references to Appendices
ST PYTHON. D.6.a.7.2.	25th Oct. contd.		Company out in front which was held up by M.G. fire from MARESCHES.	
		1836	Report from 99th Bde. that a Sergeant's patrol of 10 men, 1st R. Berks. had reached cross roads at R.4.b.7.3. at 1400. They started from MOETRY FARM and proceeded via LA CROISETTE. About 50 Germans ran away from the latter place on the approach of our patrol. No other enemy seen. Patrol was fired at by Field Guns but no M.G. or rifle fire encountered.	AppLXXXIII
		1940	2nd Div. G.80 issued. Appendix LXXXIII. Orders to units outlining the policy of VI Corps. 99th Bde. to be responsible for defence, organisation and maintenance of Corps main line. The 3rd Div. taking over the duties of advanced guard on whole Corps front.	
			No further fighting took place during the day.	
			The 99th Bde. pushed patrols out to the line LA CROISETTE - R.2.a.8.9. and established touch with Divisions on both flanks.	
			The night 25/26th Oct. passed quietly.	
			2nd Div. Locations. Appendix LXXXIV.	AppLXXXIV.
	26th Oct.		The 8th Inf. Bde. (3rd Div.) took over the outpost line on 2nd Div. front from 99th Bde, relief of troops in the outpost line was completed by 0600.	
			No infantry engagements took place during the day.	
			Troops of the 99th Bde. withdrew to the Corps main line of resistance and reorganised in depth.	

Army Form C. 2118.

WAR DIARY
INTELLIGENCE SUMMARY.
(Erase heading not required.)

Instructions regarding War Diaries and Intelligence Summaries are contained in F.S. Regs., Part II. and the Staff Manual respectively. Title pages will be prepared in manuscript.

Place	Date	Hour	Summary of Events and Information	Remarks and references to Appendices
ST PYTHON D.6.a.7.2.	26th Oct. (cont.)		Cavalry patrols operating in front of the 3rd Division during the morning reported VILLERS-POL strongly held by the enemy.	
			Hostile artillery was fairly active on our forward areas during the day, a large percentage of Blue Cross Gas being used.	
			2nd Division Locations. Appendix LXXXV.	App.LXXXV.
			2nd Division Strength Return. Appendix LXXXVI.	App.LXXXVI
	27th Oct.		Night 26/27th October passed quietly. About 25 rounds from a hostile H.V. gun fell in the vicinity of ST PYTHON between 0400 and 0515.	
		09.45	Warning order was received from VI Corps that on the night 29/30th October the 2nd Division would probably take over the duties of Advanced Guard Division from the 3rd Division - The Guards and 62nd Divisions closing up in rear.	
		13.08	Orders received from VI Corps for 3rd Division to take over the main line of resistance from 2nd Division on night 27th October. On Relief 2nd Division to be Support Division in the area ROMERIES - VERTAIN - ST PYTHON - SOLESMES - The area East of ESCARMAIN (inclusive) allotted to 3rd Division - See VI Corps G.349. Appendix LXXXVII.	Appendix LXXXVII
		13.50	6th Infantry Brigade were ordered to move two Battalions from ESCARMAIN to ROMERIES on 27th October - See 2nd Division G.105. Appendix LXXXVIII	Appendix LXXXVIII
		14.30	Units informed that 3rd Division were taking over the whole Corps front. 99th Infantry Brigade to be relieved by 76th Infantry Brigade during the night. On completion of relief 99th Infantry Brigade to move to SOLESMES - See 2nd Division G.106. Appendix LXXXIX	Appendix LXXXIX
		15.30	Units informed that Command of Artillery covering VI Corps Sector would pass to G.O.C. 3rd D.A. at 10.00 28th October. See 2nd Division G.108. Appendix XC.	App.XC.

WAR DIARY
or
INTELLIGENCE SUMMARY

(Erase heading not required.)

Army Form C. 2118.

Place	Date	Hour	Summary of Events and Information	Remarks and references to Appendices
	Oct.27th (cont.)	17.10	Two Battalions of 6th Infantry Brigade (1st King's Regt. and 2nd South Staffs.) moved from ESCARMAIN to ROMERIES. The situation remained unchanged during the day - Hostile Artillery was fairly active on our forward areas, and H.V. guns fired a few rounds into ST PYTHON.	
		19.30	Units informed that 2nd Division would probably relieve 3rd Division as Advanced Guard Division on night 29/30th October. If this relief is carried out 6th Infantry Brigade on the right and 5th Infantry Brigade on the left would relieve 8th and 76th Infantry Brigades respectively - 99th Infantry Brigade to be in reserve in ESCARMAIN. See 2nd Division GU.4/11. Appendix XCI.	App.XCI
		21.10	Relief of 99th Infantry Brigade by 76th Infantry Brigade complete - G.O.C. 3rd Division assumed Command of VI Corps Sector - 99th Infantry Brigade moved to SOLESMES.	
	28th Oct.		During the early morning and at odd intervals throughout the day ST PYTHON was shelled by hostile H.V. guns; little damage, however, resulted.	
		10.15	Orders received from VI Corps that moves and reliefs outlined in VI Corps Warning Order No.398 were postponed 24 hours. All recipients of 2nd Division GU.4/11 were notified accordingly. See VI Corps G.365. Appendix XCII.	App.XCII
			2nd Division Locations. Appendix XCIII.	App.XCIII
		22.50	Orders received from VI Corps that moves and reliefs outlined in Corps Warning Order No.398 would take place on 29/30th October. VI Corps No.G.365 cancelled. See VI Corps G.380.App.XCIV	AppXCIV
		23.25	Units informed that relief ordered in 2nd Division GU.4/11 would take place on October 29/30th - 99th Infantry Brigade to leave SOLESMES at 10.00 hours on 29th and move to ESCARMAIN, coming under the orders of 3rd Division until completion of relief. See 2nd Division G.122. Appendix XCV.	App.XCV

Army Form C. 2118.

WAR DIARY
or
INTELLIGENCE SUMMARY
(Erase heading not required.)

Instructions regarding War Diaries and Intelligence Summaries are contained in F.S. Regs., Part II. and the Staff Manual respectively. Title pages will be prepared in manuscript.

Place	Date	Hour	Summary of Events and Information	Remarks and references to Appendices
	Oct.28th (cont.)	23.30	Orders issued to 6th Infantry Brigade to relieve 8th Infantry Brigade (of 3rd Division) in the line on October 29/30th - Not to pass VERTAIN before 14.00 hours. See 2nd Division G.123. Appendix XCVI.	App.XCVI
	29th Oct.	08.45	Orders issued to 5th Infantry Brigade to relieve 76th Infantry Brigade (3rd Division) on 29th October - Not to pass VERTAIN before 15.30. See 2nd Division G.125. Appendix XCVII.	App.XCVII
		08.45	VI Corps order No.399 received and VI Corps GS.81/6. Detailed orders to Divisions regarding relief and moves. Guards and 61st Divisions to close up and become left and right Support Divisions respectively.	
		10.50	Detailed orders issued to units concerning relief of 3rd Division. See 2nd Division Order No.367. Appendix XCVIII.	App.XCVIII
		19.30	Instructions issued to units regarding policy to be adopted in the event of a withdrawal on the part of the enemy. See 2nd Division GR.4/3. Appendix XCVIIIa.	AppXCVIIIa
			Nothing of importance took place during the day and no infantry engagements took place. The relief of the 8th and 76th Infantry Brigades by the 6th and 5th Infantry Brigades was carried out without incident. Command of VI Corps Sector passed to G.O.C. 2nd Division on completion of relief at 21.10 hours.	
			There was some gas shelling of RUESNES and our forward areas during the night. 2nd Division Locations. Appendix XCIX.	App.XCIX
	30th Oct.		No change in situation of 2nd Division. Patrols operating on the Divisional front just before dawn reported no signs of enemy withdrawal. During the day hostile artillery was intermittently active on BELLE VUE Farm - PONT de BUAT - Halte in R.9.c. and MORTRY FARM. Some gas shelling of RUESNES was carried out during the afternoon. Enemy aircraft active during the day.	

Army Form C. 2118.

WAR DIARY
or
INTELLIGENCE SUMMARY

(Erase heading not required.)

Instructions regarding War Diaries and Intelligence Summaries are contained in F. S. Regs., Part II. and the Staff Manual respectively. Title pages will be prepared in manuscript.

Place	Date	Hour	Summary of Events and Information	Remarks and references to Appendices
	30th Oct. (cont.)		Our artillery was active carrying out harassing fire and counter-battery work throughout the day.	
			The following posts were reported to be held by the enemy :- R.4.c.3.8. - R.4.d.05.50. - R.4.d.6.3. and R.3.b.2.9. LA FOLIE Farm was reported to be occupied by the enemy.	
		19.30	Instructions issued to units regarding action to be taken in the event of a hostile counter-attack - No retirement to be made from our present outpost line. See 2nd Division GR.4/7. Appendix C.	App.C
			2nd Division Locations. Appendix C1.	App.C1.
			The night 30/31st October passed quietly.	
	31st Oct.		Some hostile shelling of BELLE VUE Farm and RUESNES took place during the early morning. Dawn patrols reported enemy dispositions normal on 2nd Division front and no signs of withdrawal.	
		14.30	G.O.C. and G.S.O.1 attended Conference at VI Corps Headquarters to discuss plans and details for forthcoming operations.	
			The situation on 2nd Division front remained unchanged throughout the day. Intermittent hostile shelling of RUESNES and vicinity took place. E.A. were active during the morning. Our Artillery was active during the day carrying out harassing fire and counter-battery work.	
		19.30	As a result of information from VI Corps all units were notified of changes in the Corps boundary. See 2nd Division GR.4/9. Appendix CII.	App.CII
		19.30	All units notified that the 2nd Division would be relieved in line on November 2/3rd by the Guards Division on the left and the 62nd Division on the right. See 2nd Division Warning Order No.368. Appendix CIII	App.CIII
			2nd Division Locations. Appendix CIV	App.CIV

2nd Division
War Diaries
General Staff

October 1918

"A" Form
MESSAGES AND SIGNALS.

Army Form C. 2121
(In pads of 100.)

Prefix......Code......m.	Words / Charge	This message is on a/c of
Office of Origin and Service Instructions	Sent At / To / By	......Service...... (Signature of "Franking Officer")

TO — 5 Bde.   M.G.Battn.   23rd Divn.
      6 Bde.   C.R.A.   3rd Divn.

Sender's Number: G.317   Day of Month: 1   In reply to Number: AAA

5 Bde. is attacking AT SUR L'OEUVRE and railway in J.9 at 1830 in conjunction with attack by 3rd Divn. AAA Artillery arrangements are being made by Group Commanders AAA In conjunction with attack by 24th Divn. on the left Artillery fire is being put down about S.central at about 1805

57

From: 2nd Division
Place:
Time:

The above may be forwarded as now corrected. (Z)

......Censor. Signature of Addressor or person authorised to telegraph in his name ......Col.
* This line should be erased if not required.

Order No. 1625. Wt. W3253/   P 511   27/2   H. & K. Ltd. (E. 2634).

NARRATIVE OF OPERATIONS.

2nd DIVISION.

27th September — 9th October, 1918.

1. From September 17th to September 27th the 2nd Division was in support in the Left Support Division Area with Headquarters at L'HOMME MORT, N.W. of VAULX VRAUCOURT. The 5th Brigade was in the neighbourhood of COURCELLES, 6th Brigade near ERVILLERS, and 99th Brigade about MORY and VAULX.

2. (i) On the 17th September warning instructions were received from VI Corps outlining the next operations which were to take place about the 25th September. September 27th was subsequently fixed for ZERO day.

   (ii) The Third Army was to attack in conjunction with the right of the First Army on its Left.

   (iii) The object of the attack was to drive the enemy across the CANAL DE L'ESCAUT and CANAL DE ST. QUENTIN.

3. The final plan for the attack by VI Corps was briefly as follows :-

   (i) The 3rd Division to attack on the right and the Guards Division on the left under a creeping barrage.

   (ii) The 62nd and 2nd Divisions to pass through the leading Divisions when these were expended, drive the enemy across the CANAL DE ST. QUENTIN and capture RUMILLY and the high ground in G.2.b. and d. (South of the FAUBOURG DE PARIS).

   (iii) The 62nd and 2nd Divisions were ordered to close up on ZERO minus 1 day and establish Divisional H.Q. in close proximity to the 3rd and Guards Divisions respectively. The 62nd and 2nd Divisions were to move forward from their assembly positions and follow the attack of the leading Division so as to be able to

- 2 -

pass through without delay when necessary.

(iv) Tanks were available to support the attack of the leading Divisions only.

4. (i) On the 26th September Right Brigades of the 2nd Division moved forward to assembly positions as follows :-

    6th Brigade leading Brigade - area between DEMICOURT and DOIGNIES.

    99th Brigade Support Brigade - area East of MORCHIES and North of BEAUMETZ.

    5th Brigade Reserve Brigade - about MORCHIES.

    M.G. Battalion - about MORCHIES.

(ii) Brigades were not allowed to enter MORCHIES before dark. The concentration was not complete till about 3 a.m.

(iii) Advanced Divisional Headquarters were established N. of DOIGNIES with the Guards Divisional H.Q. at 6-30 p.m. on the 26th September.

5. On the 27th September the attack commenced at 5-20 A.M. and made good progress on the VI Corps front.
At 6 a.m. the 6th Brigade moved forward and formed up East of the CANAL DU NORD in K.9.b. and d. During the advance the Brigade came under M.G. fire from the high ground W. of GRAINCOURT and some casualties were caused by an aeroplane bomb while crossing the CANAL DU NORD. The Brigade was formed up in its new positions by 10-45 a.m.
The B.G.C. 6th Brigade was in close touch with B.G.C. 3rd Guards Brigade (Guards Division) and at 11-40 a.m. acting on information received from B.G.C. 3rd Guards Brigade, the G.O.C. 6th Inf. Brigade ordered his Unit forward as follows :-

    2nd S. Staffs. L.13.a. (BEETROOT FACTORY)

    1st King's to L.7.a. (ORIVAL WOOD)

    17th R.Fusiliers and 6th T.M.B. to K.18. and K.12.
        (N. of FLESQUIERES).

This consisted of
- 2 Bdes Gds Div Arty
- 2 Bdes 2nd Div Arty
- 95th Bde RFA (21st Div)
- 14th Army Bde RHA.
- 88th Bde RGA.

All bdes with the exception of the 95th which was covering the left flank of the VI Corps from position near Demicourt were in action E of the Canal du Nord.

While this move was in progress news was received
that ORIVAL WOOD and the GRAINCOURT Line were
still held by the enemy.

The leading Battalion 6th Brigade came under heavy
M.G. fire from these positions on reaching K.12. and
K.18 and took up positions in trenches and sunken
roads N. of FLESQUIERES until an attack could be
organised.

6. The situation at about midday appears to have been as
follows:

The right of the Guards attack had reached the neighbourhood
of the BEETROOT FACTORY in L.13. where it was held up.
The left of the attack had not got on and was forming a
defensive flank to keep touch with the 63rd Division
(XVll Corps), which had been held up in front of
GRAINCOURT.

On the right the 3rd Division had captured RIBECOURT
and the 62nd was passing through and continuing the
advance on MARCOING.

At 2 p.m. the XVll Corps renewed the attack on GRAINCOURT
from the North and forced the enemy to retire.

7. (a) At 4 p.m. orders were issued for the 6th Brigade to
capture CANTAING SUPPORT. At this time it was
believed that the Guards held PREMY CHAPEL.

(b) At 5 p.m. C.R.A. 2nd Division took over Command of
the Artillery on the Divisional front. (c) The 6th Bde.
attacked under a barrage and covered by smoke.
ORIVAL WOOD and the GRAINCOURT Line were captured,
it was found that the Guards Division did not hold
PREMY CHAPEL, and a further advance to the CANTAING
SUPPORT Line was impossible without Artillery
preparation.

(d) The 6th Bde. in this advance had passed through the
3rd Guards Bde. The Command of the front passed to

- 4 -

G.O.C. 2nd Division at 10-15 p.m.

8. The position on the night 27th/28th September was as follows :-

The 6th Brigade was in the GRAINCOURT Line on the left of the Divisional front with the right flank at about K.9.c., with Headquarters at K.10.d.3.7. The 99th Brigade which meanwhile had been keeping in touch with 6th Inf. Brigade and was in support, moved up and took over the right Sector of the Divisional front in BEET TRENCH.

The 5th Brigade had moved E. of the CANAL DU NORD and was in support, with Headquarters at K.9.d.4.7 Command of the R.A. on the Divisional front had passed to C.R.A. 2nd Division at 1700 27th.

9. (a) The 99th and 6th Brigades were ordered to continue the attack at 5000 on 28th, objectives CANTAING SUPPORT and NINE WOOD. If possible the crossings over the CANAL DE L'ESCAUT were to be seized. The inter-Brigade boundary was the FLESQUIERES - PREMY CHAPEL Road to L.14.b.5.2. and thence the track.

(b) The 62nd Division was attacking at 0630 on the 28th. Arrangements were made for the right of the 99th Brigade to form a defensive flank until the 62nd Division should come up in line.

~~(c) Division on left.~~

(c) The 63rd Bde R.G.A. came under the orders of 2nd D.A. relieving 86th Bde R.G.A.

10. The plan of attack was as follows :-

11. The advance was resumed at 0515 (the 99th Bde. starting at 0445 to get up in line), the 28th and both Brigades reached the W. bank of the ST. QUENTIN CANAL without much opposition. It was impossible to continue the general advance across the CANAL as the enemy held MARCOING SWITCH strongly with Machine Guns and all the crossings were under fire.

12. One party of the King's Regiment (under Lieut-Col. D.M.KING, D.S.O.,M.C.) succeeded, however, in crossing the CANAL by the Lock Bridge at F.29.d.7.2. This party took and held the Lock Keeper's house on the Eastern bank.

13. The troops of the 99th Brigade had gained control of the existing crossings by M.G. fire and were successful in preventing the enemy from demolishing them during the night.

14. Late in the afternoon 2 Coys. of the 17th R. Fusiliers (6th Brigade) filtered across the CANAL by the Lock Bridge and by dusk had gained a footing in L.6.a. in the MARCOING line. Strong enemy resistance was met with and these 2 Coys. eventually fell back to a line just E. of the CANAL and W. of the MARCOING line. There they remained for the night.

15. On the night 28th/29th the situation was as follows :-
   (i) On the right the 99th Bde. (H.Q. at K.17.d.5.6.) held a line W. of the CANAL de ST. QUENTIN and commanded the crossings.
   (ii) On the left the 6th Brigade held the W. bank of the CANAL with 2 Coys. of the 17th R. Fusiliers E. of the CANAL.
   (iii) On the right flank of the 2nd Division the 62nd Division had taken MARCOING crossed the CANAL and River and had established a bridge-head.
   (iv) On the left, the 57th Division had advanced round GRAINCOURT forcing the enemy to retire and enabling the

~~All batteries had very good shooting at the schooling...~~

18. On the 29th the 14th Bde RHA and the 36th, 41st & 75th Bdes RFA moved forward to position in L 4c, 10a & 5c, 11a, 8, 9, & 15.

63rd Division to gain the line of the CANAL.

16- At 0500 on the 29th the attack was resumed by the 99th and 6th Inf. Bdes. On the right the 1st Royal Berks and 1st K.R.R.C. crossed the CANAL and after hard fighting succeeded in establishing themselves in MARCOING SWITCH gaining touch with the 62nd Division on the right and the 6th Inf. Bde. on the left. The 17th R. Fusiliers (6th Inf. Bde) on the left had hard fighting about MARCOING SWITCH and any attempt to advance was met with heavy and accurate M.G. fire. About midday, however, the enemy was seen retiring on the left in A.19.d. and on the right in G.2.d. Two Coys. of the 17th R. Fusiliers then advanced and captured the trench line in G.1.b. and G.2.a. and c. with many prisoners. In the evening the left was swung round to run N. and S. from G.1.b.8.5. to A.26.c.1.9. in order to gain touch with the 63rd Division.

17- In the meantime the 99th Brigade had made a joint attack with the 62nd Division with objectives G.3.c.5.0. - G.2.d.7.7. (99th Bde.) and RUMILLY (62nd Division). The 1st K.R.R.C. carried out the attack on the 2nd Divisional front and was successful but the advance on MONT SUR L'OEUVRE was held up owing to M.G. fire from RUMILLY which had not been taken by the 62nd Division. During the afternoon the 1st Royal Berks reorganised and pushed forward to the trench in G.2.a. and d. The 6th Inf. Bde. was then withdrawn and the whole Divisional front was held by the 99th Inf. Bde. with 1st K.R.R.C. on the right and 1st R. Berks on the left. In the evening the 23rd R. Fusiliers relieved the 1st K.R.R.C. in the right sub-sector.

BRIDGING. 19 Early on the morning of the 29th the advanced section of the 5th Field Coy. R.E. had constructed a footbridge over the CANAL from old German floats found lying about and a Battalion of Infantry had been got across on this Bridge.

The river and CANAL were thoroughly reconnoitred by Officers of the 5th, 226th, and 483rd Field Coys. R.E. and another footbridge was built at L.6.c.3.2. At 4 pm a pontoon bridge to take Infantry transport was completed by 226th Field Coy. R.E. at L.6.c.3.1.

The 483rd Field Coy. R.E. repaired the NOYELLES river Bridge and Bridge No. 1 and 10 and threw a new pontoon bridge (No. 17) over the CANAL.

This work was carried out steadily throughout the day under heavy shell fire and was of incalculable value to subsequent operations as well as for those in progress on the 29th.

SEPT. 30th. Owing to the attack of the 62nd Division on RUMILLY on the 29th being unsuccessful our line was withdrawn on the evening of 29th to just E. of FLOT FARM - E. of the Sunken Road in G.8.a. - G.2.d. central - 200^x W. of the MASNIERES CAMBRAI Road - A.27.c.9.1. where the 1st Royal Berks had touch with the flank Division. The 52nd Div (XVII Corps) had come in on the left of the 2nd Division relieving the elements of the 63rd and 57th Divisions which were E. of the CANAL.

On the morning of the 30th September the 23rd R. Fusiliers (99th Bde) attacked MONT SUR L'OEUVRE but were unable to make progress owing to heavy M.G. fire from RUMILLY.

At 0700 the line was withdrawn to the starting off position where it remained throughout the day.

It had now become evident that RUMILLY and MONT SUR L'OEUVRE must be captured simultaneously with RUMILLY by a concerted attack with the Division on our right and with strong Artillery support.

At 1600 orders were issued by Division for the 5th Inf. Bde. to take over the line as soon as practicable after dark on the 30th. **The relief of the 99th Bde. by the 5th**

Phase II starts here

was completed at 0100 and the 99th Bde. was withdrawn to reserve in the NINE WOOD - FLESQUIERES area.

BRIDGING
On the 30th September the 5th Field Coy. R.E. threw another footbridge across the CANAL at L.5.b.7.0. and repaired the German Bridge at L.5.d.40.45. This Bridge was rendered passable for Field Artillery. The 483rd Field Coy. reconstructed No. 10 Bridge to take 60pdrs. The 226th Field Coy. R.E. constructed a new trestle Bridge over the CANAL at L.12.c.6.2. and strengthened the River bridge at L.11.b.7.1. to take 60pdrs.

Capture of MT sur L'OEUVRE

1st. Oct.
On the morning of 1st October the Division was disposed as follows :-

        Div. H.Q. ... ... FLESQUIERES
        5th Inf. Bde. ... Line - H.Q. NOYELLES.
        6th Inf. Bde. ... Support " "
        99th Inf. Bde. ... Reserve H.Q. L.15.a.3.1.
        (West of NINE WOOD)

The 3rd Division passed through and took over from the 62nd Division during the night of September 30th/Oct. 1st and was on the right flank of the 2nd Division.
The 52nd Division (XVll) Corps was on the left.
The 5th Inf. Bde. had the 24th R. Fusiliers on the right and the 2nd H.L.I. on the left. The 52nd L.I. was in reserve. At 0600 the 52nd L.I. attacked under cover of a slow barrage to clear up the ground between MARCOING SWITCH and the high ground in G.10.d. The 3rd Division simultaneously attacked RUMILLY.
The atrack went well at first. The 3rd Division cleared the S.W. corner of RUMILLY and ensured the right flank of the 2nd Division but owing to heavy M.G. fire no progress was made beyond the road running N. and S. in G.8.d. Touch was gained with the 2nd H.L.I. on the left by patrols. During the day located enemy M.Gs. and occupied points were severely harassed by our Artillery. A minor oper-

(c) During this period 2nd DA TM personnel used a captured 15 cm How, a 21 cm How + a 10 cm H/V gun and fired 242 rounds (including (?)) on Forenville Wambaix + the Railway in G10.

(d) On 2nd October the 14th Bde RHA + 95th Bde RFA crossed the Canal de St Quentin + came into action in y1+2 + y7 + 73 respectively. On the 5th Oct the 74th + 75th Bde RFA were transferred in situ to the XVII Corps and 95th Bde RFA withdrew + rejoined the 21st Div.

- 9 -

ation by the 2nd H.L.I. at noon to clear up a M.G. nest at G.3.c.7.0. was unsuccessful owing to flanking M.G. fire.

26. The enemy still held RUMILLY except the S. and S.W. edges and the general line of the CAMBRAI - MASNIERES Road to the FAUBOURG DE PARIS, also MONT SUR L'OEUVRE. During the afternoon a further simultaneous attack on RUMILLY and MONT SUR L'OEUVRE was arranged, the objective of the 2nd Division being G.3. central - G.10. central and of the 3rd Division G.10. central - G.17. central. The 52nd Division was to attack the FAUBOURG DE PARIS 45 minutes before.

27 (a) At 1745 the 52nd Division attacked the FAUBOURG DE PARIS and at 1830 the 2nd Division and 3rd Division simultaneously attacked MONT SUR L'OEUVRE and RUMILLY. The attack was supported by an intense barrage of smoke shrapnel and H.E. and T.Ms. were used to smother and harass the M.Gs. in the Quarry at MONT SUR L'OEUVRE and the road and trench at G.3.c.4.0.

(b) By 1945 both Battalions reported that their Coys. were crossing the main road. The leading Coy. of the 24th R. Fusiliers (72 strong) took 180 of the total of 200 prisoners captured.

(c) The attack of the 52nd Division on the left was unsuccessful but the 3rd Division cleared RUMILLY and on the night Oct. 1st/2nd the 2nd Division held the main road and the trench line through G.9.d. and G.10.c. within the Divisional boundaries.

28 (a) Between Oct. 2nd and Oct. 8th this line was firmly established and on the 3rd a line of posts was established in conjunction with the 3rd Division to gain observation over the ridge N.E. of RUMILLY.

29 (b) On the night of Oct. 3rd the 5th Inf. Bde. was relieved by the 6th Inf. Bde. and handed over the above line with the exception of the post in the Signal Box on the railway at G.4.c.2.1. which had been driven in by an enemy attack

just prior to the relief. A valuable identification was secured by us on this occasion but the post was not re-established in the Signal Box.

29. Between Oct. 3rd and Oct. 8th the 6th Inf. Brigade held the line with 1st King's Regiment on the right, 2nd S. Staffs on the left and 17th R. Fusiliers in reserve (H.Q. FLOT FARM) The 5th Inf. Bde. was in support in the NOYELLES area and the 99th Inf. Bde. in reserve in the NINE WOOD - FLESQUIERES area.

30. During this period the Royal Engineers continued the work of improving and maintaining the crossing over the SCHELDT and CANAL DE ST QUENTIN.

A new trestle bridge was constructed by the 5th Field Coy. R.E. to take lorries over the river at L.5.d.3.2. This was completed by October 3rd. On the same day the 226th Field Coy. commenced 2 trestle bridges over the river at L.17.b.6.2. and 60.75 and a pontoon bridge over the CANAL at L.18.a.0.3. Maintenance of approaches and existing bridges was constantly attended to by the Coys. not actually engaged in new construction.

On the 6th October a steel girder portable road bridge of 60' span was commenced at L.11.b.6.7. by 226th Field Co. R.E. and pontoon bridge No. 23 was thrown across by 483rd Field Coy. R.E.

On the 7th, work on the girder bridge was suspended and all Coys. were engaged on the strengthening of existing bridges to take the increased transport which was expected in consequence of the imminent renewal of the advance. Ph. III - Capture of Forminiere

32.(a) On the 6th October information was received that the attack was to be resumed in the near future. Certain adjustments in Boundaries were to be made in Corps and Divisional Boundaries to enable the XVll Corps to attack from a South Westerly direction.

(b) The objectives of the 2nd Division were to be the

33(b) ←

The 75th Bde RFA moved after dark on the 7th to position E of the Canal de St Quentin.

35(b) ←

At 0504 the 41st Bde RFA advanced & came into action E of Rumilly opening fire from the new position at 0630.

SERANVILLERS - NIERGNIES Trench Line and FORENVILLE, with exploitation further East if enemy resistance weakened.

(C) The 3rd Division was to attack on the right of the 2nd Division, and the 63rd Division (XVll Corps) was to attack on the left. The 63rd Division was to pass through the troops of the 2nd Division (6th Bde.) in the line - a portion of the 57th Division (XVll Corps) which was attacking on the left of the 63rd Division was also to pass through the 6th Bde.

At 2000 on the 7th October the 99th Bde. H.Q. moved to MONT SUR L'OEUVRE and the whole Brigade marched from the NINE WOOD - FLESQUIERES area East of the CANAL forming up for the attack on a line S.E. of RUMILLY running through G.16.d. 17.c. and 23.a.

The attack on the first objective was carried out at 0430 by the 23rd R. Fusiliers on the right and the 1st K.R.R.C. on the left. The 1st R. Berks was to pass through the 23rd R. Fusiliers and advance with the 1st K.R.R.C. to capture the 2nd objective.

The first objective was reached and captured with comparatively little difficulty but re-organisation was hard to complete owing to the absence of landmarks and the consequent loss of direction of units of both the 2nd and flanking Divisions.

At 0640 the barrage protecting the first objective lifted and the 1st R. Berks and 1st K.R.R.C. advanced to attack the GREEN LINE (Main CAMBRAI - PARIS Road including FORENVILLE). On the left the attack went well, the K.R.R.C. and 1 Coy. of the 1st R. Berks reaching their objective; on the right, heavy M.G. fire was encountered from FORENVILLE and the advance was checked. The Tanks detailed to support the attack on FORENVILLE if necessary were not forthcoming, but Company Commanders continued to work forward and as the 3rd Division was approaching LA

TARGETTE the capture of FORENVILLE seemed at 0800 to be only a matter of time.

At 0815 however the situation was changed by the launching of an enemy counter-attack supported by Tanks. The main attack was delivered against the 63rd Division and lft flank of the 2nd Division from the direction of AWOINGT and 5 enemy Tanks were employed. At the same time 1 enemy Tank attacked the left of the 3rd Division between LA TARGETTE and FORENVILLE.

At first it was not realised that these Tanks were hostile (They were captured Mk. iv British Tanks) and it was not until troops of the 2nd Division saw the troops on both flanks falling back that it was realised that the Tanks were German. As both flanks were entirely exposed the 1st K.R.R.C. and the left Coy. 1st R. Berks withdrew to the RED LINE (SERANVILLERS - NIERGNIES branch line). In the meantime the hostile tanks were engaged by the 99th T.M. Battery with a captured German Light Minenwerfer and assisted by the rifle fire of the Infantry, caused the Tanks to divert from their original objective. Only 2 Tanks actually approached within 200 - 300yds of the REDLINE. One of these was driven off by fire from a Stokes Mortar which was now in action and the crew of the other was compelled to leave its Tank, and was eventually captured by the 23rd R. Fusiliers.

At 1030 the troops of both the 2nd Division 3rd and 63rd Divisions were back on the RED LINE. They were definitely established there and the enemy counter-attack had been beaten off. Attempts to renew the advance were however unsuccessful as the advancing troops of the 2nd Division came under heavy M.G. fire from both flanks.

An attack at 1500 on FORENVILLE and the GREEN LINE was unsuccessful owing to very heavy M.G. fire from both flanks especially from the neighbourhood of the CEMETERY

The 14th Bde R.H.A. moved up to position in G.17b & 18a & the 36th Bde R.F.A. to G.16a

(C) The 36th & 41st Bdes were withdrawn from the line on the night Oct 9/10 and were billetted in the Noyelles - Marcoing - Rumilly area.

in H.1.c. which when the attack was launched was believed to be in the possession of the 63rd Division. An attack by the 3rd Division on LA TARGETTE at 1300 had also been unsuccessful as and it was evident that LA TARGETTE, the high ground N. of SERANVILLERS and FORENVILLE must be attacked simultaneously to ensure success.

40. The 17th R. Fusiliers (6th Inf. Bde) had been placed at the disposal of G.O.C. 99th Inf. Bde. during the morning and the B.G.C. 99th Inf. Bde. had been verbally informed by the Divisional Commander that this Battalion might be used if necessary to assist in the capture of the GREEN objective.

41. At 1800hrs the 17th R. Fusiliers attacked in conjunction with the 3rd Division on our right, and captured FORENVILLE. At the same time the 23rd R. Fusiliers (1 Coy.) formed a defensive flank to the North and the 3rd Division took LA TARGETTE. About 60 prisoners were taken in FORENVILLE and a considerable number of light M.Gs.

42. During the night the 1st K.R.R.C. pushed out to the main road and thus completed the capture of the final objective. In the early morning the Guards Division passed through and took over from the 2nd Division on the GREEN LINE and continued the advance. The 2nd Division was (less arty) withdrawn into Corps Reserve and disposed as follows :-

    H.Q. ... ... J.10.a.3.3. DOIGNIES.
    5th Inf. Bde.   DEMICOURT AREA
    6th Inf. Bde.   CANAL DU NORD AREA
    99th Inf. Bde.   FLESQUIERES &ORIVAL WOOD
                                  AREA.

43. The Field Companies R.E. and the 10th D.C.L.I. (Pioneers) came under the orders of V1 Corps for work in the CANAL DE L'ESCAUT area.

ACCOUNT OF OPERATIONS. - 8th. OCTOBER. 1918.

The 2nd. Division took their First Objective afterwards going on tow[ards the]
Second Objective.

FORENVILLE was not taken though the K.R.Rs. on the Left of the attac[k took their]
Second Objective.

About 1000, an enemy Tank appeared from the South of FORENVILLE. It [was]
accompanied by Infantry and made for Lieut. Murphy's Machine Gun.

The Infantry on the Right of the 2nd. Division and the Left of the 3rd. Division
fell back to the First Objective.

Lieut. Murphy withdrew his Machine Gun slightly and opened fire on this Tank, when
it withdrew.

Two other Tanks were also seen at this place. The Infantry appeared to be c[om]-
pletely taken by surprise at seeing what they thought to be our Tanks firing on t[hem.]

In the evening, FORENVILLE was taken by 2nd. Division, but lost again betwee[n]
0200 and 0300 on the 9th. It was retaken however by the Guards in their advance o[n the]
9th.

The 63rd. Division on the Left were counter-attacked with a barrage and with
Tanks about 1600. The Infantry fell back but advanced again soon after.

From 1600 to dark the front line of the 63rd. Division was seen to fall back and
then go forward again four times altogether.

The only time the enemy Infantry were seen to attack the 63rd. Division was at
1600, when small parties of the enemy with Tanks were seen advancing from the direction of the Cemetery.

On each occasion that the 63rd. Division front line went forward, it appeared to
advance without reinforcements having been seen coming up.

In fact, the battle on the 63rd. Divisional front, from 1600 onwards seemed to
sway backwards and forwards, without either side being engaged very heavily.

During the whole day very heavy enemy machine gun fire came from the Railway line,
and barrages were put down at intervals on our line, usually at the junction of the
3rd. and 2nd. Divisions. For some reason the enemy seemed to make a dead set at this
part of the front.

About 1700, the enemy apparently attacked the left of the 3rd. Division, driving
the Left of this Division back a short distance. The Infantry were driven back, stated
that they could not get touch with troops on either flank, and had suffered heavily
from machine gun fire, and required reinforcements.

The 2nd. Division did not appear to be included in this attack as the only men
who came back were wounded.

The above are from the accounts given by Section Officers of the 2nd. Battalion,
M.G. Corps.

CONFIDENTIAL.

Headquarters,

2nd Division "G".

Herewith Narrative of Operations between 1st and 9th October, 1918, inclusive, in accordance with your No. G.T.1749/1 of 10/10/18.

12/10/18.

Brigadier General,
Commanding, 6th Infantry Brigade.

1. **October 1st – 2nd.**

   No change in the situation. The Brigade remainded out of the line in the vicinity of NOYELLES.

2. **October 3rd – 7th.**

   On the night of October 3rd/4th the 6th Brigade relieved the 5th Brigade in the line.
   1st KING'S Regt. took over the Right Sector; 2nd S.STAFFS Regt. the Left Sector and 17th R. FUSILIERS remained in Support in the vicinity of FLOT FARM.
   On October 4th 6th Brigade Hd.Qrs. moved to the Southern outskirts of NOYELLES.
   During this period the situation remained unaltered. New Posts were established by both the Front Line Battalions on the high ground N. of Mt SUR L'OEUVRE and N.E. of RUMILLY.
   Hostile Artillery was active at intervals on the forward area and considerable harassing fire was carried out by both sides on battery positions and back areas.

3. **October 8th.**

   At 0430 the offensive was resumed. 6th Infantry Brigade, however, did not take part in these operations, but continued to hold the line.
   During the night of October 7th/8th the 63rd (R.N.) Division formed up in 6th Brigade area, and at ZERO passed through our troops. The assembly was completed without incident, the hostile Artillery being less active than usual.
   At 0950 orders were received to place the 17th ROYAL FUSILIERS at the disposal of G.O.C. 99th Infantry Brigade. This was accordingly done and the Commanding Officer was ordered to report in person to 99th Infantry Brigade Hd.Qrs. at Mt SUR L'OEUVRE.
   At 1800 the 17th R. FUSILIERS carried out a most successful operation, capturing the Village of FORENVILLE with about 60 prisoners.
   The dispositions of 1st KING'S Regt. and 2nd S. STAFFS Regt. remained unaltered for the remainder of the day.

4. **October 9th.**

   During the morning the 6th Brigade were withdrawn to the vicinity of the CANAL Du NORD, EAST of DEMICOURT.
   Units were ordered to be clear of NOYELLES by 0930 and to concentrate at their respective Transport Lines S.W. of NINE WOOD.
   On completion of this concentration Units marched independantly to to their own billeting areas. This move was completed about 1200, Brigade Hd.Qrs. being established at K.7.d.3.0., EAST of DEMICOURT.

S.T.6524.

REPORT ON OPERATIONS from 23rd.September to 4th.October, 1918.
----- oOo -----

Reference Map.   57c. 1/40,000.

Date.	Time.	
23.Sep.		Orders were received that the Battalion would move to the RUYAULCOURT Area on 24th., and that 2 Coys. would be employed under the direction of the C.E. on the HAVRINCOURT WOOD Plank Road.
24.Sep.	9.30.a.m.	The Commanding Officer visited the C.E., VI Corps with regard to work on the Plank Road.
	10.0.a.m.	The Battalion moved off from A.15.a.1.3.
	1.0.p.m.	Halt at H.34.c.7.8. near BAPAUME, where Dinners were taken.
	4.0.p.m.	Arrived at P.3.c.5.7. near RUYAULCOURT and camped. The Battalion had marched 18 miles and only two men had fallen out, and one of those had broken his ankle. The 1st.Battalion were passed amidst scenes of great enthusiasm.
25.Sep.	6.30.a.m.	The Commanding Officer proceeded with Os.C. "Y" & "Z" Coys.to reconnoitre work.
	7.30.a.m.	Coys. arrived on work. The road was in a very bad condition, the formation having completely disappeared in places, and the construction was also somewhat faulty. In other words, it was one of the worst "Jobs" to undertake "Technically", and that portion of the road near YORKSHIRE Spoil Bank K.32.b.3.8. gave one the idea that when the "Show" came off, it would be very sticky. The enemy made the road in the vicinity of K.32.b.3.8. very uncomfortable on several occasions during the day.
	5.0.p.m.	The Coys.returned to Camp.
26.Sep.	6.30.a.m.	"Y" & "Z" Coys.proceeded to work on the Plank Road. (It is well to state here that several extraneous jobs, such as unloading lorries, burying horses, and helping vehicles in distress occurred.) The day passed off without event, except for the shelling of that portion of the work near YORKSHIRE Spoil Bank.
	5.0.p.m.	Final instructions had been received from Division, and were communicated to O.C.Coys. for the attack on the 27th.
27.Sep.	5.20.a.m.	ZERO.
	6.0.a.m.	"Y" & "Z" Coys. were on the HAVRINCOURT WOOD Plank Road and "X" Coy. assembled about K.27.a.3.7. whilst the Commanding Officer and O.C. "X" Coy. proceeded forward to reconnoitre tracks (see attached map.)
	7.30.a.m.	It was very evident that both tracks could be started at once. Therefore 1 Platoon proceeded to work on each.

● To Division only.

Date.	Time.	
27.Sep.	9.30.a.m.	No.1 Track was through to K.16.d.central.

No.2 Track was through to K.10.central where it was held up by enemy Machine Gun fire from K.11.c.3.9.

This Platoon (under 2/Lt: A.A.R.OXFORD) on No.2 Track had a considerable amount of sport, and claim to have killed quite a

3.0.p.m. considerable number of the enemy. The enemy were eventually knocked out of this stronghold, but this late eviction held up the work considerably.

The two remaining platoons of this Coy. were sent up, and pushed both tracks through to within 500 yards of the front line, which was just west of ORIVAL WOOD.

Great credit is due to 2/Lts: A.A.R. OXFORD and A.L.POTTER for the able way in which they handled their platoons, and with the speed in which they carried out their tasks.

"Y" and "Z" Coys. relieved one another alternately on the track through HAVRINCOURT WOOD during the night.

28.Sep. 6.0.a.m. "Y" and "Z" Coys. relieved one another throughout the day on the Plank Road.

Several direct hits had been obtained on the Plank Road during the day, one of which completely obliterated it, but thanks to the good work put in by "Y" Coy. practically no stoppage of traffic took place.

"X" Coy. finished the tracks to ORIVAL WOOD and maintained same.

10.0.a.m. It had become apparent that the enemy had moved right away, as there was very little hostile fire of any sort.

6.0.p.m. The two Coys.which had been working on the Plank Road rejoined the Battalion for work under the Division.

29.Sep. 8.0.a.m. Battalion H.Q.moved to K.18.b.7.4.
Coys. to positions as follows :-
"X" Coy. to Bank in K.12.b.5.9 - K.12.b.7.2.
"Y" "   " K.12.c.7.0.
"Z" "   " trenches K.18.a. & b.

10.0.a.m. "Z" Coy. proceeded straight to work clearing the GRAINCOURT, L.8.b - FLESQUIERES Road. The situation was quiet. A great deal of work had to be done on the road.

4.30.p.m. Two platoons of "X" Coy.were detailed to make a track to cross pontoon bridge at about L.6.c.5.0. However, on the arrival of the Commanding Officer and O.C.Coy. at this spot, it was found that 1 platoon would be sufficient. The other Platoon was therefore utilised to make a dry weather track from L.6.c.5.0. to G.2.c.4.4. Again 2/Lt:OXFORD showed sound judgement, and what was best of all "He got a move on" and got the men to work quickly. The shelling at this time was considerable in this area.

- 3 -

Date.	Time.	
30.Sep.	7.0.a.m.	"X" Coy.remained in reserve for tracks. "Y" Coy.worked on clearing road from L.9.d.1.0. to NOYELLES. 2 Platoons "Z" Coy.commenced approaches to bridges at L.6.c.2.4., L.6.c.2.1., L.5.b.6.2., L.6.c.2.5., L.5.d.3.2., L.12.d.5.2. 2 Platoons "Z" Coy.remained in reserve.

1.Oct.

Work was continued on roads and bridge approaches as follows :-
(a) FLESQUIERES, L.13.central, L.8.b.2.8., L.9.d.1.0., NOYELLES.
(b) L.9.d.1.0., L.15.b.9.0., NOYELLES and bridge approaches at L.6.c.2.4., L.6.c.2.1., L.5.b.6.2., L.6.c.2.5., L.5.d.3.2., L.12.d.5.2.

2.Oct.

Work continued on roads and bridge approaches as follows :-
(a) FLESQUIERES, L.13.central, L.8.b.2.8., L.9.d.1.0., NOYELLES.
(b) L.9.d.1.0., L.15.b.9.0., NOYELLES and bridge approaches at L.6.c.2.4., L.6.c.2.1., L.5.b.6.2., L.6.c.2.5., L.5.d.3.2., L.12.d.5.2.

3.Oct.

Work continued on roads and bridge approaches as follows :-
(a) FLESQUIERES, L.13.central, L.8.b.2.8., L.9.d.1.0., NOYELLES.
(b) L.9.d.1.0., L.15.b.9.0., NOYELLES, and bridge approaches at L.6.c.2.4., L.6.c.2.1., L.5.b.6.2., L.6.c.2.5., L.5.d.3.2., L.12.d.5.2.

4.Oct.

Work continued on roads and bridge approaches as follows :-
(a) FLESQUIERES, L.13.central, L.8.b.2.8., L.9.d.1.0., NOYELLES.
(b) L.9.d.1.0., L.15.b.9.0., NOYELLES, and bridge approaches at L.6.c.2.4., L.6.c.2.1., L.5.b.6.2. L.6.c.2.5., L.5.d.3.2., L.12.d.5.2.

The approaches to the bridges included 100 yds. of brush wood road and 300 yds of Plank Road.

The Repair to roads consisted of a large amount of revetment, and a great many cubic feet of earth to be moved. The work was, in fact, exactly what a Pioneer Battalion was trained for, and there is no doubt about the interest taken in it by all ranks.

The following letter of appreciation was received from the Divisional Commander, and has been communicated to all concerned :-

"2nd.Division No.G.S.1751.

O.C., 10/D.C.L.I.

Please convey my great appreciation and thanks to all ranks of the 10th.Battn.D.C.L.I.for the exceptionally good work they have done on road repairs and the construction of approaches to the bridges over the River ESCAUT and Canal de ST QUENTIN. I am well aware of the difficult conditions under which work has had to be carried out owing to the enemy's constant shelling.

(Sd.) C.E.PEREIRA, Major-General,
Commanding 2nd.Division.

5/10/18."

--------oOo--------

REMARKS and SUGGESTIONS arising from the Actions
27th. September / 3rd. October, 1918.
-------- oOo --------

1. It would appear that when it has been decided that a track should be made from a certain place to a certain place that the time to commence work be left to the Commanding Officer of the Pioneer Battalion, who can arrange to be either on the spot, or have his representative there.
This will save a lot of time from the present arrangement. Under the present arrangement, Artillery often make the tracks first and the Pioneers improve them, which appears to be directly reverse to that which it ought to be.

2. That it should be borne in mind that Pioneers were technically trained in England for roadmaking, Light Bridging, Rail-Road making, etc., and that there are still left a large percentage of those who were originally trained in addition to Officers who have since been trained in England, and that these qualifications should be encouraged and developed.

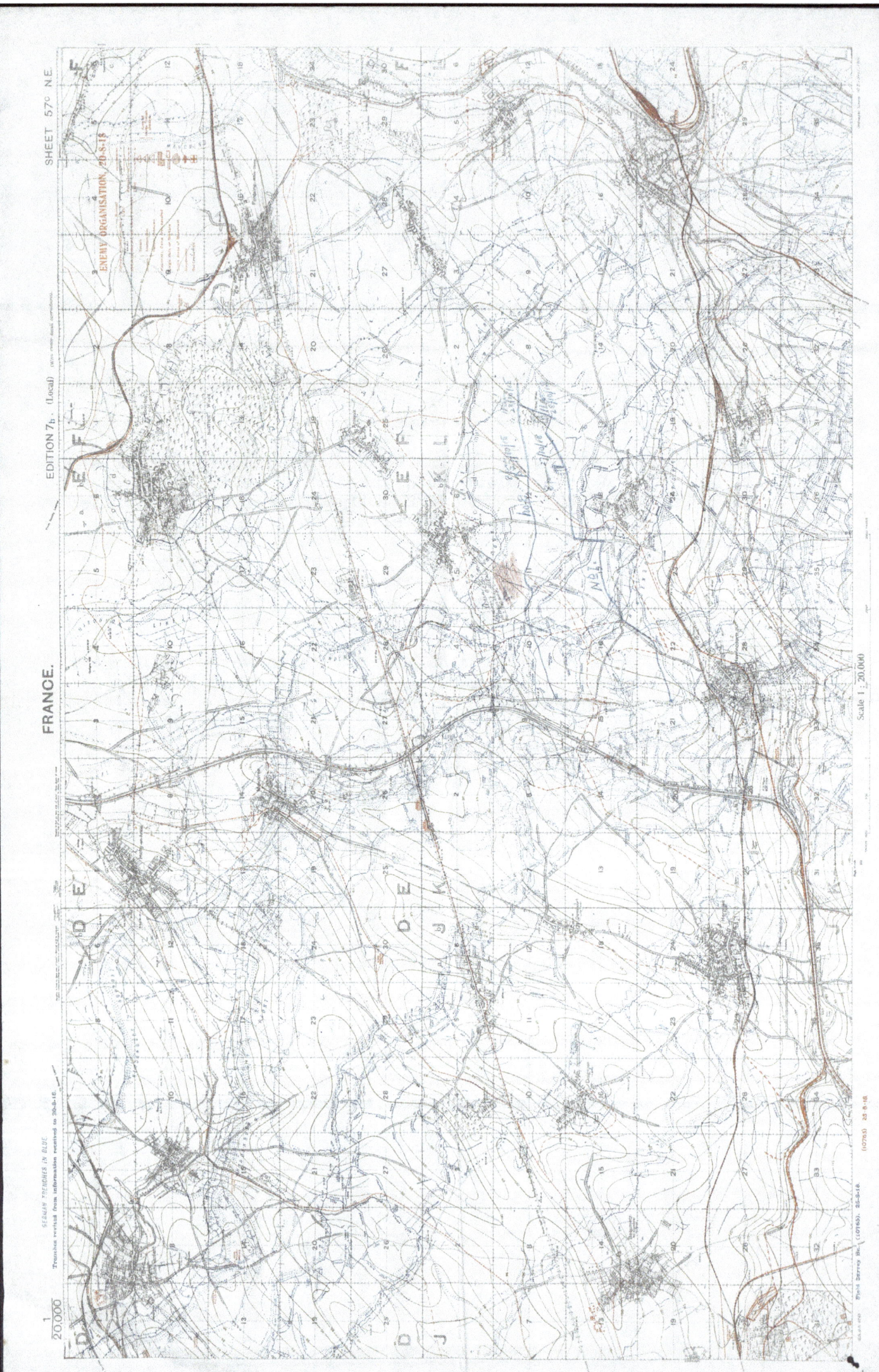

REPORT ON OPERATIONS FROM 27th SEPTEMBER, 1918.

September 27th.   At 5 p.m. C.R.A., 2nd Division took over command
of the Artillery supporting the Guards and 2nd
Divisions.
    This consisted of :-
        2 Brigades Guards Div. Artillery.
        2 Brigades 2nd Div. Artillery.
        95th Brigade, R.F.A. (21st Division).
        14th (A) Brigade, R.H.A.

    With the exception of the 95th Brigade, R.F.A.,
who were still covering the left flank of the VI
Corps attack from positions N.E. of DEMICOURT, all
Brigades were at this time in action East of the
CANAL DU NORD. Their further advance was hampered
by the enemy being still in GRAINCOURT, but later
41st and 74th Brigades came into action in K 17 a.&.c.

September 28th.   All Artillery (less 95th Brigade, R.F.A. and
2 Batteries 36th Brigade, R.F.A.) supported attack
of 6th Infantry Brigade at 5.20 a.m., the 5 Brigades
moving later into action in area NINE WOOD - ORIVAL
WOOD.
    63rd Brigade, R.G.A. came under orders of 2nd
D.A. relieving 88th Brigade, R.G.A.

September 29th.   All batteries had very good shooting during the
day at enemy retiring over ridge North of MT. SUR
L'OEUVRE.
    The following Brigades moved forward during the
29th :-
        14th Bde, R.H.A. to L 8 & 9.
        36th Bde, R.F.A. to L 15.
        41st Bde, R.F.A. to L 5 c & 11 a.
        75th Bde, R.F.A. to L 4 c and 10 a.

    During the night of the 29th, 99th Infantry
Brigade crossed Canal under cover of a barrage put
down by 36th Brigade, R.F.A.
    6th Infantry Brigade crossed Canal without any
barrage.

September 30th.   All Brigades supported attack on MT. SUR L'OEUVRE
and high ground to North.
    Positions of Brigades :-
        14th Bde, R.H.A.   L 8 & 9.
        36th Bde, R.F.A.   L 15.
        41st Bde, R.F.A.   L 5 c & 11 a.
        74th Bde, R.F.A.   L 5 d.
        75th Bde, R.F.A.   L 4 c & 10 a.

October 1st.   3rd Division on right attacked RUMILLY and this
Division MONT SUR L'OEUVRE and high ground to N,
in early morning. These objectives were not, however,
captured until the evening. 3rd Division's barrage
starting 1745 and ours 1830. All Brigades attached
to 2nd D.A. took part except 95th Brigade, R.F.A.
Prisoners statement shewed that enemy casualties,
due to Stokes and Artillery fire, were very heavy.

October 2nd.   14th Bde, R.H.A. and 95th Brigade, R.F.A. came
into action across CANAL DE ST. QUENTIN in G 1 and
2 and in G 7 and 13, respectively.

October 3rd.
2nd D.A.
Instructions
No 1 attached.

    47th Battery, 41st Bde, R.F.A. has one section in
action L 8 b. Instructions re relief of 6th Inf. Bde,
Artillery co-operation with tanks and establishment
of Smoke Shell received.

October 4th.	VI Corps order to withdraw 74th and 75th Bdes, R.F.A. to DOIGNIES received. 15th Battery, 36th Brigade put an Anti-Tank Section in G 14. 14th Brigade, R.H.A. withdraw 400th Battery to L 11 d.
October 5th. 2nd D.A. Instructions No. 2 attached.	VI Corps order re 74th and 75th Bdes, R.F.A. postponed, and the former Battery transferred in "Situ" to XVII Corps. 95th Brigade withdrew during night to 21st Division. 2nd D.A. Instructions No. 2 re regrouping of Brigades, issued.
October 6th. 2nd D.A. Instructions No.3 attached.	36th Brigade, R.F.A. occupy positions vacated by 95th Brigade, R.F.A. 2nd D.A. Instructions No. 3 - Warning Order re attack by 99th Infantry Brigade, Artillery support etc, issued. All batteries of 63rd Brigade, R.G.A. now across Canal, G 7 b & d. 63rd Brigade, R.G.A. engaged trench line W. of SERANVILLERS and N. 2nd D.A. Trench Mortar personnel fired 242 rounds from 2nd - 6th October, with one 15cm How, one 21cm How and one 10cm H.V.Gun (captured from enemy) on FORENVILLE, WAMBAIX, Railway G 10, Quarries H 10 a and other targets, including 24 rounds BLUE CROSS GAS on WAMBAIX.

2nd Divisional Artillery Instructions No.1.

3rd October 1918.

1. The 6th Infantry Brigade will relieve the 5th Infantry Bde. in the line to-night.

   Artillery arrangements will be as follows :-

   Liaison Officer with 6th Infantry Brigade, Lt-Col.P.BARTON, D.S.O.

   RIGHT GROUP. Lieut-Col. Wickham, D.S.O.
   14th Brigade R.H.A.
   36th Brigade R.F.A.
   95th Brigade R.F.A.

   LEFT GROUP. Lieut-Col. P.BARTON, D.S.O.
   41st Brigade R.F.A.
   74th Brigade R.F.A.
   75th Brigade R.F.A.

2. **CO-OPERATION WITH TANKS.**

   When the advance is resumed, Tanks will be allotted to the Units which are likely to meet with the most opposition.
   When the Infantry are seriously held up, the Tanks will be called up, their advance being protected by Smoke and by Artillery fire on the Objective.
   When the advance is again resumed, Tanks will fall in their place behind.
   The sections or single guns pushed forward with the Infantry will be used in close co-operation with the Tanks to overcome any opposition.

3. **SMOKE.**

   There is still difficulty in obtaining Smoke Shell, and the greatest economy must be exercised in using them.
   Every Battery will in future keep up an Establishment of 120 Smoke Shell which for moving operations should be distributed equally amongst the wagons. No Smoke will be fired in future during stationary warfare without authority of the C.R.A., unless required for some urgent operation.

4. **Bridges.**

   New Bridges ready at 11 a.m. to-day fit for Field Artillery :-

   Trestle Bridge L 17 b 55.20.
   Pontoon Bridge L 18 a 0.2
   Weldon Trestle Bridge, L 17 b 60.35

   Major R.A.
   Brigade Major R.A. 2nd Division.

Distribution :-

2nd Division "G"	41st Bde. R.F.A.	R.A.VI Corps.
5th Infantry Bde.	74th "	H.A.VI Corps.
6th "	75th "	2nd D.A.C.
99th "	95th "	A.R.P.
14th Bde.R.H.A.	63rd " R.G.A.	
36th "		

SECRET

2nd Divisional Artillery Instructions No 2.

October 5th, 1918.

1. The 74th and 75th Brigades R.F.A. and Guards D.A.C. will be withdrawn from the line to-day. *postponed*

2. The Field Artillery supporting the 2nd Division will be re-grouped as under :-

    RIGHT GROUP   Lieut-Col. Wickham D.S.O.

        14th Brigade R.H.A.
        95th Brigade R.F.A.

    LEFT GROUP   Lieut-Col. P. BARTON, D.S.O.

        36th Brigade R.F.A.
        41st Brigade R.F.A.

Liaison Officer with 6th Infantry Bde. Headquarters, Lieut-Colonel P. BARTON, D.S.O.

3. Lieut-Col. Barton will make necessary arrangements for changes in S.O.S. lines from 10 a.m. to-day.

4. Two Anti-Tank guns will be placed in action in "Silent" positions West of RUMILLY by 36th Brigade R.F.A. to-night, to cover the high ground North of MT. SUR L'OEUVRE and Valley East of it.

                                      Major R.A.
                      Brigade Major R.A. 2nd Division.

Distribution:-

2nd Div. "G"	74th Bde. R.F.A.	63rd Bde. R.G.A.
5th Infantry Bde.	75th ,,	S.C.R.A.
6th ,,	95th ,,	R.O.R.A.
99th ,,	Guards D.A.C.	R.A. Signals.
14th Bde. R.H.A.	2nd D.A.C.	
36th Bde. R.F.A.		
41st ,,	R.A. VI Corps.	

S E C R E T.

2nd Divisional Artillery Instructions No.3.

W A R N I N G   O R D E R

October 6th, 1918.

1. The 99th Infantry Brigade will attack in conjunction with Divisions on Right and Left before daylight on the morning of October 7th, the final objective being about the main road in H 7 b and FORENVILLE.

   Lieut-Col. A.A.GOSCHEN, D.S.O., will be Liaison Officer with G.O.C. 99th Infantry Brigade.

2. Artillery support will be as under :-
   - 14th Bde.R.H.A. - Creeping Barrage from present positions.
   - 36th Bde.R.F.A. - Creeping Barrage from 95th Bde.R.F.A. positions in G 7 b and d.
   - 41st Bde.R.F.A. - Creeping Barrage from present positions, up to about G 12 b and d, then advance.
   - 75th Bde.R.F.A. - Creeping Barrage beyond about G 12 b & d, from positions in G 8 d and 14 b.

3. 74th Bde.R.F.A. will be transferred in situ to XVII Corps to-day, under orders of VI Corps.

4. 36th and 75th Bdes.R.F.A. will move into new positions (As in para. 2) to-night and be ready to open fire by 3 a.m. to-morrow morning.

5. **Ammunition.** Probable requirements :-
   - 14th Bde, R.H.A.) 350 rds. per gun,
   - 36th Bde. R.F.A.) to include 50 Smoke per 18-pr gun.
   - 41st Bde. R.F.A. 200 rds.per gun (No Smoke)
   - 75th Bde. R.F.A. (250 rds.per gun,to include 50 (Smoke per 18-pr.

6. O.C.36th Bde. will detail a section of guns to be in action behind the crest about G 2 d to take advantage of fleeting opportunities.

   The Section in G 14 c will not be required for Anti-tank purposes after this morning.

7. Brigades, please acknowledge by wire.

Brigade Major R.A.2nd Div.

Major R.A.

Distribution:-
2nd Division "G"	36th Bde. R.F.A.	R.A.VI Corps.
5th Infantry Bde.	41st Bde. R.F.A.	H.A.VI Corps.
6th Infantry Bde.	75th Bde. R.F.A.	2nd D.A.C.
99th Infantry Bde	74th Bde. R.F.A.	Guards D.A.C.
14th Bde.R.H.A.	63rd Bde. R.G.A.	A.R.P.

S.C.R.A.
R.O.R.A.
R.A.Sigs.
Diary.

S.T.6771.

REPORT ON OPERATIONS from 5th. to 9th. OCTOBER, 1918 (inclusive).
-------- oOo --------

Reference Map. 57C.

Date.	Time.	
Oct.5th.	0600. to 1800.	Work was continued on repair of roads and bridge approaches. "X" and "Y" Coys. did particularly well on the road from L.8.b.2.8., via L.15.b.9.0. through NINE WOOD to NOYELLES. The greater portion of this road is sunken with dugouts, and the spoil had been thrown on to the road, and in some places was as much as 16 ft. deep. The road was cleared, and widened 8 feet. "X" Coy. did some splendid work on that portion of the road just West of NINE WOOD. At the commencement of work, the road was impassable to anything more than limbers, but by the 7th. a first-class road for lorries had been built. The revetting of the large craters was very well done. No.26433, Sgt.W.A.M.STRIBLEY, M.M. distinguished himself on this work.
Oct.6th.	0600. to 1800.	Continued work on bridge approaches and main roads. About this time, the bridge approaches became fairly "hot corners" and the good work put in by "Z" Coy. was very noticeable; the fascine and brick road at L.12.c.0.8. to L.12.c.3.6. and the Plank Road at L.6.c.1.2. to L.6.c.3.2. were marked places, but all ranks stuck to their work.
Oct.7th.	0600. to 1800.	Work was continued on main roads and bridge approaches, "Z" Coy. experiencing quite exciting times. It is calculated that the Plank Road would be ready for use on the night of Oct: 8th.
Oct.8th.	0600.	"X" and "Y" Coys. continued work on the main road through NINE WOOD. "Z" Coy. were detailed to finish the Plank Road, and to keep the bridge approaches in repair. 2/Lt: A.G.L.BURTON was detailed with his Platoon to help anyone in trouble either with bridges or bridge approaches.
	0630.	2/Lt: E.J.C.LINSCOTT reported that the canal level had fallen, and that the site for the plank road was under water. This naturally stopped the plank road. Efforts were made to open up drains to the river, and relieve the flooded area, but without much success, as it was found that a sluice had sprung a leak, and that the leak was greater than the amount that could be got away. 2/Lt: A.G.L.BURTON, whilst on patrol, found the Pontoon Bridge at L.6.c.25.20 sunk partly by a gun and a limber, which had gone over the edge, and partly owing to the fact that the level of the canal had dropped about 3 ft. 6.ins.
	0730.	2/Lt: A.G.L.BURTON organized his platoon and proceeded to relieve the pontoon of the gun and limber, and other extraneous matter. This took
	1030.	till about 1030, and during the whole time the enemy continued to shell the spot. Great credit is due to 2/Lt: A.G.L.BURTON, 22422, Sgt.C.BENNETTS 11125, Sgt.B.HUTTON, 24886, Pte.F.BULLOCK and 260234, Pte.G.HEAD for the absolutely great work they put in, as, apart from shelling and machine

(1.)   P.T.O.

- 2 -

Date.	Time.	
Oct. 8th.	1030	gun fire from the air, they stood a good chance of being drowned.
	1130.	The Pontoon had been taken down, the pontoons emptied out and everything placed in position ready to reconstruct.

It must be remembered that Pioneers are not trained to any great degree in Pontooning, so perhaps they may be pardoned for taking slightly longer over the job than the scheduled time. The fact remains, however,

1300: that the bridge was re-erected solely by Pioneers, and that it was only when the chesses was being placed in position that a party of R.Es. (who had been working higher up stream) were able to come down and lend a hand.

During this time 2/Lt:E.J.C.LINSCOTT was battling with the water which had flooded his job, (Plank Road.)

The Commanding Officer decided to build the plank road on brushwood, and this proved very effective, though of course the road took much longer to complete. It was complete on the 12th., and covered with flaked granite. It is well to remember that for the greater period during construction the ground was under water to a depth of at least a foot. The job was disappointing, in that it was not done in the time anticipated, also that the former portion of the plank road, which was laid previous to the flood looked hopeless, although as was afterwards found out it was perfectly sound with the exception of one place of about 5 yards, which had to be done again. 2/Lt:E.J.C.LINSCOTT and his platoon did exceptionally well on this road, and had benefitted by what they had learned on the plank road they made to the approach of the bridge over the river at L.6.c.1.2. to L.6.c 3.2. The one great thing to remember on those kind of occasions is the dont get down-hearted, but do something to take place of that which you have failed to finish owing to causes over which you have not control. Remember, although you may not do the next best thing the thing you do, so long as it meets the occasion, is good enough - improvements can come later. But get the Transport and Guns through on some kind of a makeshift. Speed first, then improvements when time permits.

Oct.9th.   The Division was relieved, and the Battalion worked for CORPS.

-------- oOo --------

Summary of Operations for period 1st - 9th October 1918.
2nd Signal Coy. R.E.

Two exchanges were being worked by 2nd Signal Coy after the move to Flesquieres - a main exchange at Div.Hq. Flesquieres and a sub exchange at Rear Div.Hq. Demicourt. These exchanges were in direct communication with 6th Corps and with each other. From the Flesquieres exchange lines had been laid to 62nd Div. (on right) and 63rd Div. (on left). Communication to Brigades was as follows;- (1) The original cable laid during the advance from Division to all three Brigades. (2) A cable to 5th Brigade in Noyelles laid on 30th Sept. An officer and 6 men were living at Noyelles ready to carry these lines forward should any further moves take place.

1st October. All lines were patrolled and improved. Cross country cables were frequently broken by transport etc.

2nd October. A cable (YB1) was laid to 52nd Division (who had relieved 63rd Div) headquarters at Cantaing Mill. During the evening the forward party laid a line from Noyelles to Mont sur L'Oeuvre. This was used by Brigade in line to Battalions. A second cable was laid by Brigade signals.

3rd October. A cable (YB2) was laid from Div. to 6th Brigade in Noyelles. The forward party was withdrawn from Noyelles.

4th and 5th October. No new lines were laid. A patrol was sent out on each line to Brigades every day. The lines were holding well and the only trouble was from occasional shelling in Noyelles.

6th October. A line was laid from 5th Brigade to 6th Brigade. The 6th Brigade laid a third cable to Mont sur L'Oeuvre. There was frequent trouble during the whole period through enemy shellfire on canal and river crossings.

7th October. The 63rd Division established a Headquarters in Nine Wood. A line was laid from 2nd Div. to 63rd Div. and another line was laid from 63rd Div. to 6th Brigade in Noyelles. The 99th Brigade Hq. opened up at Mont sur L'Oeuvre during the evening and were in direct communication with 2nd Div. and 6th Brigade. Two linemen were sent up to 99th Brigade and four linemen to 6th Brigade to maintain the lines between Noyelles and Mont sur L'Oeuvre. A wireless station was erected at Mont sur L'Oeuvre and was in direct communication with 2nd Division.

8th October. 99th Brigade attacked. From zero until about 08.00 hours there was continual trouble through hostile shelling, chiefly between Noyelles and Mont sur L'Oeuvre. Every line was broken time after time but owing to the work of the linemen, communication to Brigades was maintained throughout the operations.

9th October. 2nd Division was relieved by Guards Division. 2nd Div.Hq. closed at Flesquieres at 10.00 hours and opened up at Doignies at same hour. All Brigades were in direct communication with Demicourt Exchange which was in direct communication with 2nd Div.Exchange at Doignies.

Flank communications, both between Divisions and Brigades was again proved to be most important, especially during the battle on Oct.8th. On several occasions when direct communication was broken it was possible to speak to Brigades through the lines of a flank Division and by mutual working of Divisions, uninterrupted communication was maintained to the front Brigades.

Wireless. A mobile wireless set was carried with each Brigade and set up when Brigades were in the line, giving direct communication with Div.Hq. They were useful on occasions.

Pigeons. Were again useful.

Visual. Communication was established between Mont sur L'Oeuvre and a station at N.E. corner of Nine Wood which was in telephonic communication with 6th Brigade. It was useful on occasions.

October 17/18.

Diagram of Communications – 2nd Division
Night of Oct 8th 1918

2nd Signal Coy. R.E.

- Brigades of 63rd Division
- Mont Sur L'Oeuvre ZII
- Battalions of Gth Bde
- Adv. 63rd Div. Nine Wood
- Noyelles ZF
- Visual Station
- Noyelles ZE
- 24th Div. Exchange Cantaing Mill
- 57th Div.
- 3rd Div.
- Rear YB Deniécourt
- M.G. Batt"
- Y.B. Flesquières
- 3rd Div. Flesquières
- Corps

Lines: YB.5, YB.3, YB.2, YB.1, FC.6, DA.70

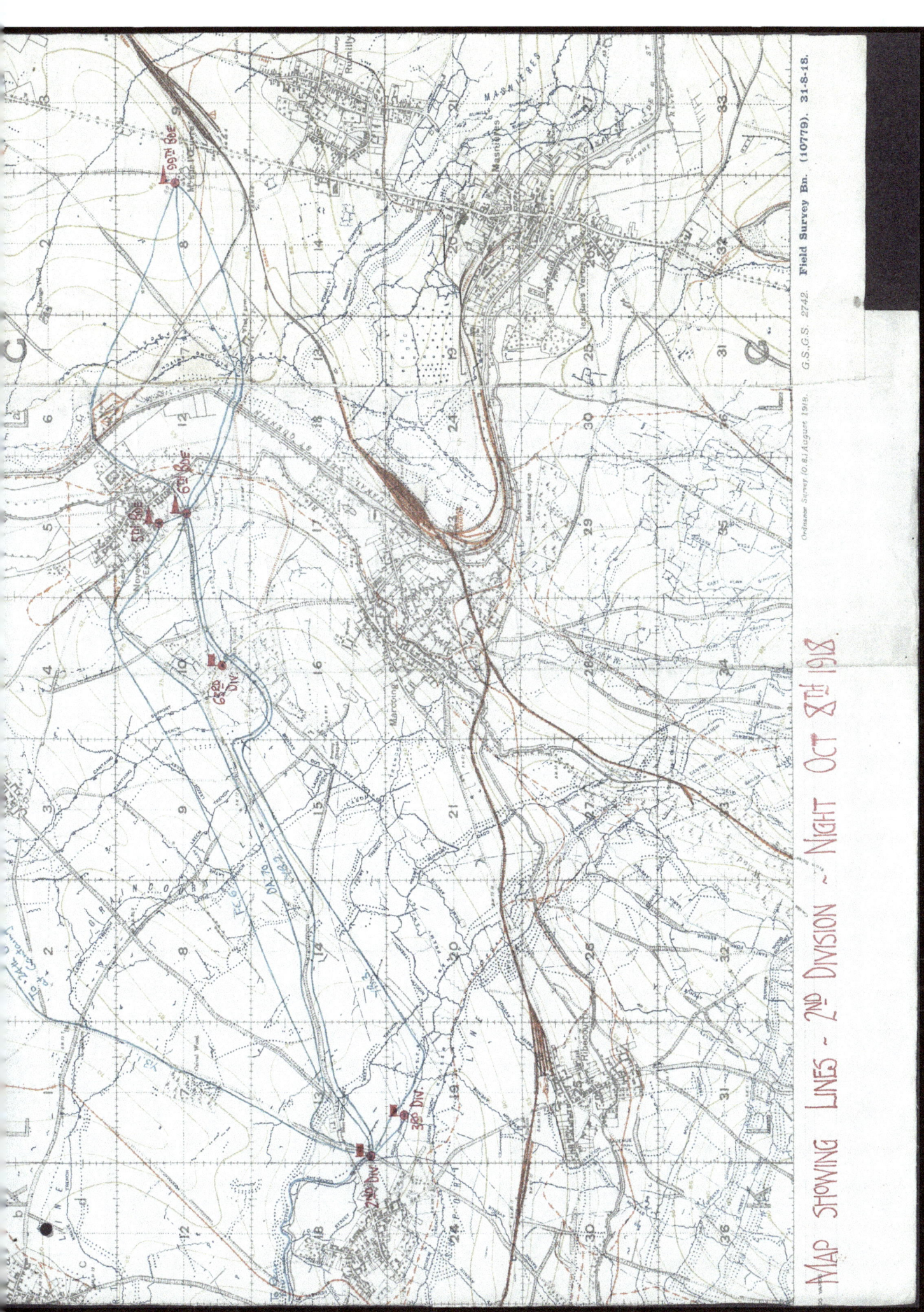

"A" Form.
MESSAGES AND SIGNALS.

Army Form C. 2121.
(In pads of 100.)

TO	2nd Division

Sender's Number.	Day of Month.	In reply to Number.	
G 38	1		AAA

Orders for to-morrow Oct 2nd AAA Pressure on the enemy is to be maintained all along the front AAA 4 Corps are continuing their advance against the high ground N. of NESDAIN AAA 17th Corps after clearing the FAUBOURG DE PARIS and the main road in A.27 are advancing on AWOINGT capturing NIERGNIES on the way AAA 3rd and 2nd Divs. if the objective of the attack that was carried at 1830 this evening is not entirely successful will complete that operation and then will gain ground to the line SERANVILLERS NIERGNIES maintaining touch with the enemy AAA Oxford Hussars less detachments will assemble at RIBECOURT at 0730 coming under the orders of G.O.C. 3rd Division AAA O.C. Oxford Hussars will report at H.Q. 3rd Div. at 0730 AAA ACKNOWLEDGE AAA Addressed 2nd and 3rd Divs.

From: Sixth Corps.
Place:
Time: 2025

"A" Form
MESSAGES AND SIGNALS.

Army Form C. 2121
(in pads of 100.)
No. of Message ....

Prefix......... Code....... ......m.	Words.	Charge.		This message is on a/c of :	Recd. at............m.
Office of Origin and Service Instructions.	Sent				Date
	At............m.			...............Service	From......
	To..........				
	By.........			(Signature of "Franking Officer.")	By......

TO
  8 Bde.   O.R.A.   92nd Div.
  6 Bde.   O.R.B.   A.D.M.S. 5th Corps

Sender's Number.   Day of Month.   In reply to Number.   AAA

Orders for tomorrow are to keep up pressure on
enemy and maintain touch AAA 3rd Div. will
be advancing their line in conjunction with
5th Corps which is advancing against high
ground north of LANDAS AAA On left 107th
Bde. is ordered to reach line of railway
A.28.d preparatory to forward move on
MARCHIES AAA 6th Bde. will occupy ridge in
A.10.d up to boundary relieving troops of 3rd
Div. will push out patrols to gain touch
with enemy and will be prepared to push
forward in conjunction with 3rd Div. on
right and 62nd Div. on left AAA 6th Bde.
to acknowledge

From   62nd Division
Place
Time   22.35

The above may be forwarded as now corrected.   (Z)

A Form
MESSAGES AND SIGNALS.

Army Form C. 2121
(In pads of 100.)

TO: 5th Bde 6th Bde 99th Bde ~~URA URE~~
M.G. Battn. Signals 3rd Division 52nd Div
"Q" A.D.M.S.

Sender's Number.	Day of Month.	In reply to Number.	
G 244	2		AAA

5th Bde will establish posts on the line G.11.c.0.0. G.10.central Railway in G.4.c. connecting with the line being established by the 3rd Division through G.17.central AAA O.C. M.G. Battalion will arrange to cover this line with M.G. fire AAA The position is to be organised in depth and the above line is to be held in case of an attack AAA 5th Bde. and M.G. Battalion to acknowledge

From: 2nd Division
Place:
Time: 1840.

"A" Form.
MESSAGES AND SIGNALS.

Army Form C. 2121.
(In pads of 100.)

TO: 2nd Division

Sender's Number: G 58
Day of Month: 2

One Field Coy. 2nd Division will be placed at the disposal of C.E. 6th Corps for work on bridge at NOYELLES under C.R.E. 2nd Division starting work tomorrow 3rd AAA ACKNOWLEDGE AAA Addsd. 2nd Division reptd. C.E. and Q.

From: Sixth Corps
Time: 1855

"A" Form.
MESSAGES AND SIGNALS.

Army Form C. 2121.
(In pads of 100.)

TO: 2nd Division

Sender's Number.	Day of Month.	In reply to Number.	
G 57	2		AAA

Orders for 3rd October AAA 3rd and 2nd Divs. will make good following general line AAA read through G.23.d. and b. L'EPINE cross roads and spur running through G.17.a. and G.10.cent. thence G.4.c.0.0. G.3.cent. and will reorganise in depth AAA Touch will be maintained with the enemy by patrols and advantage taken of any weakening of the enemy to gain ground to the East AAA orders are being issued by 4th Corps AAA 17th Corps is endeavouring to capture the Fbg de Paris and the main road in A.27 to-night and will probably advance towards NIERGNIES late in the day tomorrow AAA Ox Hussars will assemble at RIBECOURT at 0800 hrs and will come under the orders of G.O.C. 3rd Division AAA ACKNOWLEDGE AAA Addsd. 2nd 3rd Divs. Oxf. Hussars Adv. 3rd Army 4th Corps Adv. 17th Corps 12th Sqdn. R.A.F. Corps H.A. and R.A. reptd. list B.

From: ~~2nd Division~~ Sixth Corps

Time: 1910 hrs.

"A" Form
MESSAGES AND SIGNALS.

Army Form C. 2121
(In pads of 100.)

Prefix	Code	m.	Words	Charge	This message is on a/c of:		Recd. at......m.
Office of Origin and Service Instructions			Sent			Service.	Date.........
			At......m.				From
			To				
			By		(Signature of "Franking Officer")		By

TO:
5th Bde CRA   AMDS   "Q" Signals 6th Corps
6th Bde CRE   3rd Div.   62nd Div.
99th Bde M.G. Batt.   63rd HA Bde.

Sender's Number.	Day of Month.	In reply to Number.	AAA
G 283	3		

6th Bde. will relieve 5th Bde. in the
forward area to-night October 3rd/4th aaa
Details of relief to be arranged between
Brigadiers aaa Headquarters 5th and 6th
Bdes. will remain as at present aaa Lieut-
Col. MARTIN will take over Command of
Artillery in the forward area at 1900
aaa a Liaison Officer from M.G. Battalion
will be attached to 6th Bde. from 2100
aaa On relief Battalions of 5th Bde. will
occupy the area vacated by 6th Bde. aaa
5th Bde. will then be supporting Brigade
aaa 5th and 6th Bdes. to acknowledge.

From
Place 2nd Division
Time

The above may be forwarded as now corrected.   (Z)

Censor.   Signature of Addressor or person authorised to telegraph in his name
* This line should be erased if not required.

Order No. 1625. Wt. W3253/ P 511. 27/2. H. & K., Ltd. (E. 2634).

"A" Form
MESSAGES AND SIGNALS.

Army Form C.2121.
(in pads of 100.)

Appendix VIY

TO: 5th Bde. 6th Bde. 99th Bde. M.G. Battalion
    C. R. A.

Sender's Number.	Day of Month.	In reply to Number.	AAA
G 245	5		

Reference G 244 posts will be established to-night by 5th Bde. independently of the 3rd Division at approximately G.11.c.0.0. G.10.central existing post at G.10.d.5.4. will be maintained AAA A similar line of posts will be established between G.5.central and existing advanced post in G.11.c.3.1. AAA These posts will be handed over to 6th Bde. on relief and will be strengthened on the following night October 4th/5th by 6th Bde. AAA 5th and 6th Bdes to ACKNOWLEDGE.

From: 2nd Division
Place:
Time:

"A" Form.
MESSAGES AND SIGNALS.

Army Form C. 2121.
(In pads of 100.)

APPENDIX IX

TO:
5th Bde 6th Bde 99th Bde C.R.A. C.R.E.
M.G.Batt Signals ADMS "Q" 3rd Division
52nd Division D.C.L.I.

Sender's Number.	Day of Month.	In reply to Number.	
G 267	3		AAA

WARNING ORDER AAA The Army on our right has made a successful advance and the Cavalry were expected to pass through between 1200 and 1400 AAA In the event of Cavalry having a decisive success 3rd Division will attack SERANVILLERS N.Z. Division co-operating to the South AAA 2nd Division will form a defensive flank for 3rd Division AAA Brigade holding the line will extend its right approximately G.10.central G.12.c.0.0. AAA 99th Bde. will extend this line to H.8.c.0.0. and seize FORENVILLE moving to its position by S. of RUMILLY and L'EPINE G.23.b.1.8. AAA Brigade bivouaced near NOYELLES will move one Battalion to East of CANAL to Support trenches in G.8.

Place: 2nd Division
Time: 1700

(Z)

(Sgd) P.J. MACHESY
Major GS

"A" Form.
MESSAGES AND SIGNALS.

Army Form C. 2121.
(In pads of 100.)

5th Bde 6th Bde 99vh Bde CRA CRE M.G.Batt Signals ADMS "Q" 3rd Division 52nd Div. D.C.L.I.	TO

Sender's Number.	Day of Month.	In reply to Number.	AAA
G 270	3		

Reference WARNING ORDER G 267 AAA The operation referred to will not take place for 24 hours and if ordered will be at dawn.

2nd Division

1835

Sgd. P.J.MACHESY
Major GS

"A" Form.
MESSAGES AND SIGNALS.

Army Form C. 2121.
(In pads of 100.)

TO: 2nd Division

Sender's Number: G 88
Day of Month: 3
In reply to Number:
AAA

Orders for October 4th AAA Divs. in the line will take every opportunity of gaining ground to the East should the enemy show signs of weakening owing to the operations further South AAA 2nd and 3rd Divs. will continue to make plans for the operation outlined to them by telephone this afternoon so that the operation can be carried out at short notice when ordered AAA Ox. Hussars (less detachments) will be prepared to move from their camp at one hours notice after 0700hrs. AAA ACKNOWLEDGE AAA Addsd. 2nd 3rd Divs. Adv. 3rd Army 4th Corps Adv. 17th Corps 12th Sqdn. R.A.F. Ox. Hussars R.A. H.A. reptd. remainder List B.

From: Sixth Corps
Place:
Time: 2000 hrs.

"A" Form
MESSAGES AND SIGNALS.

Army Form
(In pads of 100.)

Appendix XII DIARY

TO: 2nd Divn.

Sender's Number: G108
Day of Month: 4

AAA

Operations as outlined in 6th Corps G.S.80/105 of 3rd Oct. to Divl. Commdrs is cancelled for the present aaa ACKNOWLEDGE.

From: 6th Corps

"A" Form.
MESSAGES AND SIGNALS.

Army Form C. 2121.
(In pads of 100.)

TO	2nd Division

Sender's Number.	Day of Month.	In reply to Number.	
G 119	5		A A A

Patrols of 5th and 4th Corps have crossed the CANAL on whole front AAA 4th Corps have ordered N.Z. Division to make good the MASNIERES line through M.18 - M.12 - M.6 and then to move forward by bounds to the line HURTEBISE FARM N.14.d. - ESNES - ESNES MILL 3rd Division will keep touch with the left of N.Z. Division AAA both 3rd and 2nd Divns. will take immediate advantage of any signs of withdrawal on the part of the enemy AAA Oxf. Hussars will remain under the orders of G.O.C. 3rd Division AAA ACKNOWLEDGE AAA Addsd. 3rd 2nd Divns. R.A. H.A. 4th Corps Adv. 17th Corps Adv. 3rd Army Oxf. Hussars 12 Squad R.A.F. reptd. remainder List B.

From	Sixth Corps
Place	
Time	1325 hrs.

...NALS.

Army Form C. 2121
(In pads of 100.)

TO: 2nd Division

Sender's Number.	Day of Month.	In reply to Number.	
H 190	5		AAA

COPY DIARY *Alexander*

O.C. 95th Bde R.F.A. will report to C.R.A. 21st Division tonight at EQUANCOURT aaa O.C. 34th Army Bde R.F.A. will report tonight to C.R.A. 38th Division near EPEHY F.1.b.8.0 sheet 62c aaa 6th Corps car will pick up above C.Os at 2nd Divl. Arty H.Q. at 23.59 hours aaa Batteries of 95th Bde will march to-night to W.10 central sheet 57c and bivouac near 94th Bde R.F.A. wagon lines aaa Route METZ FINS HEUDECOURT aaa Batteries of 34th Army Bde R.F.A. will march tonight to X 24 c near OSSUS WOOD sheet 57c and bivouac near 121 Bde or 122 Bde R.F.A. wagon lines aaa Route RIBECOURT TRESCAULT GOUZEAUCOURT HEUDECOURT PEIZIERES X 24 c aaa A guide from 38th Div Arty will await arrival of Batteries 34th Army Bde from 0500 hours 6th Oct Cross Roads northern extremity PEIZIERES W.30.'.4.4. sheet 57c aaa 2nd and 3rd Divns to acknowledge.

MESSAGES AND SIGNALS.

Army Form C. 2121
(In pads of 100.)

DIARY

TO: 2nd Division

Sender's Number.	Day of Month.	In reply to Number.	AAA
H191	5		

74 Bde R.F.A. H.Q. L.7.b.0.4. Batteries in action about L.5.d. will be transferred in situ to 17 Corps for forthcoming operation and is to be attached 57 Divn. aaa

From: 6th Corps
Place:
Time: 2430

"G" Diary

2nd DIVISION.

Appendix XV

STRENGTH RETURN MADE UP TO 12 NOON SATURDAY 5th OCTOBER 1918.

UNIT.	"A" Strength excluding attached.		"B" Not present with the Unit and not at disposal of the G.O. included in Column "A".		"A" minus "B" Available fighting Strength, including Personnel of Battn. Transport & Q.M's Stores.	
	Offrs.	O.R.	Offrs.	O.R.	Offrs.	O.R.
5th INFANTRY BRIGADE.						
24th Royal Fusiliers.	40	755	11	160	29	595
2nd Oxf. & Bucks L.I.	34	738	9	127	25	611
2nd Highland L.I.	31	691	9	103	22	588
Total Brigade.	105	2184	29	390	76	1794
6th INFANTRY BRIGADE.						
17th Royal Fusiliers.	33	650	11	122	22	528
1st King's Regiment.	30	695	9	110	21	585
2nd S. Staffs Regt.	34	762	14	118	20	644
Total Brigade.	97	2107	34	350	63	1757
99th INFANTRY BRIGADE.						
23rd Royal Fusiliers.	34	738	6	120	28	618
1st Royal Berks Regt.	36	781	11	122	25	659
1st K.R.Rifle Corps.	32	754	11	124	21	630
Total Brigade.	102	2273	28	366	74	1907
Pioneer Battalion.						
10th D.C.L.I.	32	806	10	59	22	747
TOTAL DIVISION.	336	7370	101	1165	235	6205
No. 2 Bn. M.G.Corps.	45	853	4	75	41	778

Major General,
Commanding 2nd Division.

Army Form C. 2121
(In pads of 100.)

...ND SIGNALS.

Prefix...Code...m.	Words	Charge.	This message is on a/c of :	Recd. at...m.
Office of Origin and Service Instructions	Sent At...m.		*Service*	Date...
Place...	To		DIARY	From...
...	By		(Signature of "Franking Officer")	By...

TO 2nd Div.

Sender's Number.	Day of Month.	In reply to Number.	AAA
G130	6		

of 6th Corps preliminary order 337 aaa
Date is postponed 24 hours aaa ACKNOWLEDGE

From: 6th Corps
Place:
Time: 1255

"A" Form.
MESSAGES AND SIGNALS.

Army Form C. 2121.
(In pads of 100.)

TO	2nd Division.		
Sender's Number.	Day of Month.	In reply to Number.	
G140	6		A A A

Following from 3rd Army aaa In view of a rumour that the Central Powers have asked for an armistice it is possible that the enemy may attempt fraternisation and movement of troops under cover of the white flag aaa No notice is to be taken of white flag except as laid down in F.S.R. part 1 Cahp 5 section 85 aaa Any enemy attempting to fraternise are to be made prisoners aaa Ends.

ACKNOWLEDGE.

From: VI Corps
Place:
Time: 1455

TO	99th Bde ~~63rd Div.~~ C.R.E. 3rd Div.		
Sender's Number. G321	Day of Month. 6	In reply to Number.	AAA

C.R.E. will detail a party of R.E. of Pioneers under an officer to meet representatives of Battns of 99th Bde and of Brigade Headquarters at the Bridge over the ESCAUT River L.11.d.8.2 at 8 am Oct 7th aaa This party will mark out a track to be used by the Brigade and will be responsible for completing the work to the satisfaction of G.O.C. 99th Bde AAA The track will run S. of FLOT FARM South of and not inclusive of level crossing G.8.d.5.0. on to road leading through RUMILLY in G.18.central aaa Add 99th Bde and C.R.E. rptd 3rd and 63rd Divns

From	2nd Div.
Place	
Time	1920

Copy No.........

2nd Division Order No. 361.

6th October, 1918.

SECRET

1. The offensive will be continued on October 8th.
   The 9th Brigade, 3rd Division, will be attacking on the Right of the 2nd Division, and the 188th Brigade, 63rd Division on the Left.
   After the capture of the second objective, the Guards Division is moving forward to capture the third objective and eventually will take over the whole of the VI Corps front.
   Boundaries and objectives are shewn on the map issued with this Order.

2. The 99th Brigade (Headquarters MT. SUR L'OEUVRE G.8.d.1.9) will at ZERO be formed up on the general line G.17.c.7.0. - G.17.a.0.5, will pass through troops of the 3rd Division and will attack and capture the first and second objectives.
   There will be a pause of 44 minutes on the first objective.

3. Artillery arrangements are as follows :-

   (a) Bombardment of selected points by Heavy and Field Artillery. Selected points were indicated to C.R.A., 2nd Division on October 6th.

   (b) Creeping barrage opening at ZERO on the line G.17.d.75.15 - G.17.a.8.8. joining up with the barrage of flank Divisions. This barrage will dwell on the opening line for 10 minutes, then will creep forward at the rate of 100yds. in 4 minutes.

   (c) On reaching the first objective at ZERO plus 86 a protective barrage will be formed for 44 minutes, creeping forward again after that time at 100yds. in 4 minutes.

   (d) On reaching the second objective at ZERO plus 178 a protective barrage will be put down.

4. Two Tanks of 'C' Company (Major RICHARDSON) 12th Battn. Tanks will co-operate in the capture of the second objective. These Tanks will assemble at about G.21.central, which should be reached by ZERO, and will follow in rear of the Reserve Battalion 99th Brigade. Their role is :-

   (a) To assist in the capture of FORENVILLE.

   (b) Should part of the 99th Brigade be held up before reaching FORENVILLE, to assist the advance, subsequently to co-operate in the attack on FORENVILLE.

5. 99th Brigade will use the following Bridges over the ESCAUT RIVER and CANAL on the night of October 7th/8th :-

P.T.O.

- 2 -

Bridge L.11.d.8.1. over River.

Bridge L.12.c.7.2. over Canal.

These Bridges will be reserved for 99th Brigade from 2200 October 7th.

The following route will be used by 99th Brigade East of the CANAL ST QUENTIN -

South of FLOT FARM, crossing railway South and not inclusive of level crossing G.8.d.5.0, thence through RUMILLY by the road through G.15.central.

Instructions regarding roads to be used West of ESCAUT RIVER will be issued later.

6. O.C. 2nd M.G. Battalion will arrange to support the attack of the 99th Brigade.

7. Contact aeroplanes will call for flares at

    Z plus 115

    Z plus 200

The signal to denote the assembly of the enemy for counter-attack is the dropping of a Red smoke Bomb over the place where the enemy is seen.

8. "Success Signals" (three white lights) will be fired on reaching the first and second objectives.

9. O.C. Signals will arrange to synchronise watches with 99th Brigade and G.R.A. on the afternoon of Z minus 1 day.

10. The 6th Brigade will continue to hold the present line. After the attacking troops of the 63rd and 57th Divisions have passed through orders will be issued for the concentration and withdrawal of the 6th Brigade and Machine Guns covering the present Divisional front.

11. After the Guards Division has taken over the Corps front the 2nd Division will be withdrawn. Separate instructions will be issued.

12. ACKNOWLEDGE.

Issued at 2200 to:-

E R Clayton
Lieut-Colonel,
General Staff, 2nd Division.

Distribution overleaf.

Distribution :-

Copy No. 1	to	5th Inf. Brigade *
2		6th Inf. Brigade *
3		99th Inf. Brigade *
4		No. 2 M.G. Battalion *
5		C.R.A.
6		C.R.E. *
7		2nd Signal Co. *
8		10th D.C.L.I.
9		3rd Division
10		63rd Division
11		57th Division
12		63rd Bde. R.G.A.
13		VI Corps
14		"Q" 2nd Division *
15		A.D.M.S. *
16		D.A.P.M.
17		12th Tank Battalion
18		'C' Coy. 12th Tank Battalion.
19-23		G.S. Records.

* <u>Map issued.</u>

Appendix XX

Copy No........
6th October 1918.

2nd Division Instructions No. 1 (to accompany 2nd Division Order No. 361).

Crossings over ESCAULT RIVER and CANAL.

1. All bridges North of L.11 central L.12.central are allotted to 63rd Division from noon on the 7th October, when the maintenance of these bridges is being taken over by C.R.E., 63rd Division.

2. The following crossings will be available for 2nd Division :-

A	Bridge 19 L.17.b.55.25 to Pontoon Bridge 21 L.18.a. 05.25	Infantry in Fours and Field Arty.	Return traffic
B	Bridge 20 L.17.b.65.25 to Pontoon Bridge about L.18.a.30.55.	- do -	Return traffic Pontoon bridge to be constructed on 7th inst.
C	Bridge 1 L.11.d.80.15 to Bridge 10 L.12.c.70.20	Traffic up to 60pdrs. inclusive.	Forward traffic

3. Route 'C' is reserved for forward traffic from 1700 7th October.
Routes 'A' and 'B' are reserved for return traffic from 1700 7th October.

4. Route 'C' to be clear for 99th Inf. Brigade from 2200 on 7th October.
In the event of a bridge on Route 'C' being damaged and impassable, 99th Inf. Brigade can use Route 'A' or Route 'B' in a forward direction.

E R Clayton
Lieut-Colonel,
General Staff, 2nd Division.

Issued to :-

Copy No. 1 to 5th Brigade
2 6th Brigade
3 99th Brigade
4 No. 2 M.G. Battalion
5 C.R.A.
6 C.R.E.
7 2nd Signal Co.
8 10th D.C.L.I.
9 3rd Division
10 to 63rd Division
11 57th Division
12 63rd Bde. R.G.A.
13 VI Corps
14 "Q" 2nd Division
15 A.D.M.S.
16 D.A.P.M.
17 12th Tank Battalion
18 'C' Coy. 12th Tank Bn

To Accompany Instructions No 1

L.2.a.7.2.
Foot bridge to take Infy in file

L.5.d.12. Foot bridge to take Infy & Cavalry

L.5.a.3.7. Trestle Bridge to take 60 pdrs.

L.5.a.1.3. Broken Trestle Bridge to take Infy

L.6.c.1.4 Broken Trestle Bridge to take Infy

L.5.d.0.9. Pontoon Bridge to take Infy
L.6.c.1.1. Pont du Noielles. Site for proposed new bridge, one 60' Span 226" to be constructed by 226th Fld Coy RE
L.6.c.2.5-2.6. Broken Bridge to take Infy

L.5.a.3.3. Destroyed to be reconstructed by 5th Fld Coy RE (in hand)

L.5.a.4.0. Destroyed

L.6.c.3.2. Pontoon Bridge to be strengthened by 5th Fld Coy RE to take Lorries - heavy Pontoon Bridge

L.11.b.6.7. Trestle Bridge to take Fld Artillery - to be demolished & replaced by 60' Span by 226th Fld Coy RE

NOYELLES

L.11.b.7.5. Footbridge to take Infy in file

L.11.a.8.2. Trestle Bridge to take 60 pdrs.

L.12.a.7.2. Footbridge

L.11.d.8.8. Light Rly Bridge destroyed Impassable

Trestle Bridge

L.11.a.8.2. Trestle Bridge to take Infy in fours 60 Pounder

L.12.c.7.2. Trestle Bridge to take 60 Pounder   C

L.17.b.6.9.3. Trestle Bridge to take Infy in fours

To be constructed 7.10.18   B

L.17.b.6.2. Trestle Bridge to take Infantry in fours   A

L.17.b.5.9. Broken Bridge to take Infy in fours

Scale 1:10,000

"A" Form.
MESSAGES AND SIGNALS.

Army Form C. 2121.
(In pads of 100.)
No. of Message..........

Prefix ...... Code .... m.	Words.	Charge.	This message is on a/c of:	Recd. at ...... m
Office of Origin and Service Instructions.				Date........
SECRET	Sent At .... m. To ...... By		...... Service. (Signature of "Franking Officer.")	From ...... By ......

TO | 5th Bde 6th Bde 99th Bde M.G.Battn.
   | CRA CRE Signals DCLI "C" ADMS DAPM

| Sender's Number. | Day of Month. | In reply to Number. | |
| "C" Coy. | 12th | Tank Battalion | AAA |

G 338 | 7 | | |

Reference 2nd Division Order 361 of 6th
October 1918 AAA ZERO HOUR will be at
04.30 on 8th October. AAA ACKNOWLEDGE

From
Place 2nd Division
Time

SECRET

Appendix XXIII

2nd DIVISION ORDER No.362.

Copy No.......

7th October, 1918.

With reference to 2nd Division Order No.361, para.11.

1. On relief by the Guards Division, the 2nd Division will be withdrawn to the area between BOIS DE L'ORIVAL and DEMICOURT and will become Left Reserve Division in the VI Corps.

2. Headquarters will be as under:-

   Divisional Headquarters J.10.a (DOIGNIES).

   5th Inf. Bde.   K.7.c.2.6 now occupied by 1st Guards Brigade.
   6th   "   "   K.7.d.3.0   "   "   3rd   "   "
   99th "   "   L.13.c.1.3   "   "   2nd Div. H.Q.

3. Areas are being allotted by 2nd Division 'Q'.

4. Orders regarding the move from the present area will be issued later.

5. Acknowledge.

E R Clayton
Lieut. Colonel,
General Staff, 2nd Division.

Issued at 1130.

Copy No. 1 to 5th Inf. Bde.
     2   6th Inf. Bde.
     3   99th Inf. Bde.
     4   2/M.G.Battn.
     5   C.R.A.   15 VI Corps.
     6   C.R.E.   16 63rd Bde. R.G.A.
     7   2/Signal Coy.   17 'Q' 2nd Divn.
     8   10/D.C.L.I.   18 A.D.M.S.
     9   2/Div. Train.   19 D.G.O.
    10   Guards Division. 20 S.S.O.
    11   3rd Division.   21 D.A.P.M.
    12   62nd Division.   22 D.A.D.V.S.
    13   63rd Division.   23 D.A.D.O.S.
    14   57th Division.   24-28 G.S.Records.

Appendix XXIV

SECRET

ADDENDUM No.1 to 2nd Division Order No.361.

7th October, 1917.

1. The forming up place of the 99th Inf. Bde. will be as follows:-
    Right Battn. G.23.a.8.8 to G.17.c.4.4.
    Left Battn. G.16.d.8.2 to G.16.b.3.1.

2. Reference para. 5 of 2nd Division Order No.361, the following routes are available for the 99th Inf. Bde. on the night of October 7/8th -

    (a) From cross roads L.15.b through NINE WOOD to cross roads L.10.d.6.7 - cross roads L.11.d.2.9 thence by road leading South through L.11.d to bridge at L.11.d.8.2.

    (b) Road on South side of NINE WOOD.

3. The opening barrage line of the 57th and 63rd Divisions is as follows- G.17.a.8.8 - G.4.c.5.3 - G.3.b.0.3.
    6th Brigade will arrange to have all posts withdrawn 300^x behind this line by zero - 30 minutes.

4. Headquarters will be as follows:-

    99th Inf. Bde.   MT SUR L'OEUVRE
    188th Inf. Bde. (63rd Divn.) MT SUR L'OEUVRE
    189th Inf. Bde. (63rd Divn.)   -do-
    9th Inf. Bde. (3rd Divn.) G.20.d.7.2.

5. Acknowledge.

P.J. Mackesy, Major
  ft. Lieut. Colonel,
General Staff, 2nd Division.

13.00.

Issued to

5th Inf. Bde.   63rd Division.
6th Inf. Bde.   57th Division.
99th Inf. Bde.   VI Corps.
2/M.G.Battn.   63rd Bde. R.G.A.
C.R.A.   'Q' 2nd Divn.
C.R.E.   A.D.M.S.
2/Signal Coy.   D.A.P.M.
10/D.C.L.I.   12th Tank Battn.
3rd Division.

LOCATIONS 2ND DIVISION

Appendix [signature]   8th October, 1918.

2nd Division H.Q. Adv.	L.13.c.1.3.		
Rear	DEMICOURT		
2nd Signal Coy.	L.13.c.1.3.		
C.R.A.	L.13.c.2.3.	74th Bde R.F.A.	L.7.b.0.4.
36th Bde R.F.A.	L.15.a.3.0.	75th Bde R.F.A.	L.5.c.2.4.
41st Bde R.F.A.	L.11.b.3.0.	95th Bde R.F.A.	L.17.a.1.7.
14th Army Bde R.H.A.	L.11.b.2.4.		
C.R.E.	L.13.c.1.3.		
5th Field Coy	F.25.d.0.2.		
226th Field Coy.	L.13.d.1.7.		
483rd Field Coy.	L.14.a.3.5.		
5th Inf Brigade.	L.11.b.1.3.		
24th Royal Fusiliers)			
2nd Oxf & Bucks L.I.)	MOYELLES AREA		
2nd H.L.I.)			
6th Inf. Brigade.	L.11.d.2.9.		
17th Royal Fusiliers)	FLOT FARM G.7.d.2.3.		
1st King's Regt)	MT. SUR L'OEUVRE G.9.a.0.0.		
2nd S. Staffs Regt.)			
		Battle H.Q. Mt. Sur L'Oeuvre	
99th Inf. Brigade.	L.15.a.3.0.		
23rd Royal Fusiliers	L.15.b.1.1.		
1sr Royal Berks Regt.	L.9.c.1.3.		
1st K.R.R.C.	L.10.d.1.3.		
M.G.Battalion.	K.18.d.9.5.		
10th D.C.L.I.(Pioneers)	K.18.b.7.4.		
A.D.M.S.	L.13.c.1.3.		
Main Dressing Stn.	K.15.b.5.3.		
Advanced Dressing Stn.	L.11.d.4.5.		
Amb. Car Posts	G.8.d.5.0.	G.7.b.8.0.	
Divl.Rest Station	J.13.b.2.1.		
63rd Bde R.G.A.,H.Q.	L.13.c.45.30.		
VI Corps H.A. H.Q.	K.24.b.4.8.		
P.O.W.Cage	L.11.d.5.5.		
57th Div.,H.Q.	F.15.c.0.4.	3rd Div., H.Q.	L.19.a.6.7.
170th Bde	F.19.c.6.1.	8th Bde	L.23.d.4.3.
171st Bde	F.21.b.6.2.	9th Bde	L.27.b.0.4.
172nd Bde	F.22.b.7.2.	Battle H.Q.G.20.d.7.2.	
63rd Div.,H.Q.	L.1.c.4.9.	76th Bde	L.22.a.6.7.
188th Bde	F.26.a.2.1.)	Battle H.Q.MT SUR L'OEUVRE	
189th Bde	E.30.b.5.6.)		
190th Bde	L.2.a.8.3.		

W. 2. Taggart Capt.
for Lieut. Colonel,
General Staff, 2nd Division.

7/10/18.

APPENDIX XVI

APPENDIX

MESSAGE FORM.

To _____   Nº _____

{ Note – Either give map reference or mark your position by an "X" on the map on back.

1. I am at _____
2. My line runs _____
3. My Platoon/Company is at _____ and is consolidating
4. My Platoon/Company is at _____ and has consolidated
5. Am held up by (a) M.G (b) Wire at _____ (State where you are.)
6. Enemy holding strong point _____
7. I am in touch with _____ on Right / Left
8. I am not in touch with _____ on Right / Left
9. Am shelled from _____
10. Am in need of _____

11. Counter-attack forming at _____
12. Hostile (a) Battery (b) Machine Gun (c) Trench Mortar active at _____
13. Reinforcements wanted at _____
14. I estimate my present strength at _____ Rifles
15. Have captured _____
16. Prisoners belong to _____
17. Add any other useful information here.

Time _____ m   Name _____
Date _____ 1918.   Platoon _____
                       Company _____
                       Battalion _____

(A) Carry no maps or papers which may be of value to the Enemy.

(B) Give no information if captured, except the following which you are bound to give Name and Rank.

(C) Collect all captured maps and papers and send them in at once.

"A" Form
MESSAGES AND SIGNALS.

Army Form C. 2121.
(in pads of 100.)
No. of Message ....

Prefix........ Code........m.	Words.	Charge.			Recd. at........m.
Office of Origin and Service Instructions.	Sent		This message is on a/c of:		Date............
	At........m.		............Service		From............
	To		XXVI		
	By		(Signature of "Franking Officer.")	By	

TO { 6" Bde
     99" Bde.

Sender's Number.	Day of Month.	In reply to Number.	AAA
G.379	8		

6" Bde will put reserve Battn at disposal of 99" Bde forthwith aaa. OC. Battn to report to O.C. 99" Bde at once.

From 2" Div
Place
Time 09.50

Sigd. E.J.R. CLAYTON

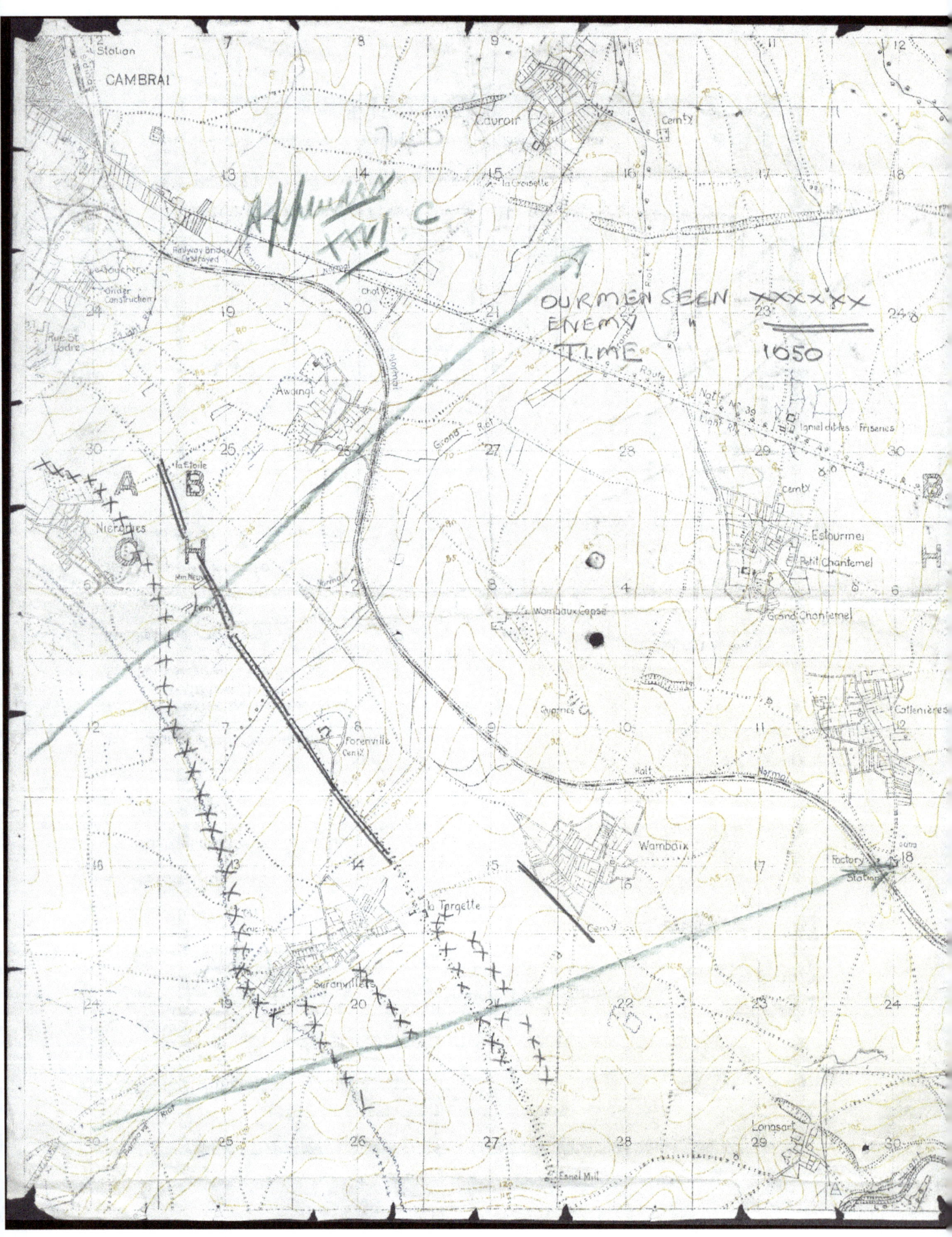

To _____ No _____

{ Note:- Either give map reference or mark
your position by an 'X' on the map
on back.

1. I am at _____
2. My line runs _____
3. My Platoon/Company is at _____ and is consolidating
4. My Platoon/Company is at _____ and has consolidated
5. Am held up by (a) M.G (b) Wire at _____ (State where you are)
6. Enemy holding strong point _____
7. I am in touch with _____ on Right/Left at
8. I am not in touch with _____ on Right/Left
9. Am shelled from _____
10. Am in need of _____
11. Counter-attack forming at _____
12. Hostile (a) Battery (b) Machine Gun (c) Trench Mortar active at
13. Reinforcements wanted at _____
14. I estimate my present strength at _____ Rifles
15. Have captured _____
16. Prisoners belong to _____
17. Add any other useful information here. _____

Time _____ m   Name _____
Platoon _____
Date _____ 1918.   Company _____
Battalion _____

(A) Carry no maps or papers which may be of value to the Enemy.

(B) Give no information if captured, except the following which you are bound to give Name and Rank.

(C) Collect all captured maps and papers and send them in at once.

"A" Form.
MESSAGES AND SIGNALS.

Army Form C. 2121.
(In pads of 100.)

TO 3rd Divn. 63rd Divn. 6th Corps

Sender's Number.	Day of Month.	In reply to Number.	
G 387	8		AAA

Attack on FORENVILLE and Green Line in 2nd Divn. area will be resumed at 1500 under a creeping barrage.

From 2nd Divn.
Place
Time 1420.

(Sd.) E.R.Clayton,
Lt.Col.

"A" Form.
MESSAGES AND SIGNALS.

Army Form C. 2121.

TO	2nd Divn.		
Sender's Number.	Day of Month.	In reply to Number.	
G197	8		AAA

4th Corps reports it has captured GREEN Objective AAA 17th Corps has captured NIERGNIES and is now moving fresh Bde forward to complete capture of GREEN Objective AAA 3rd Div has captured SERANVILLERS and 2nd Divn. hold the RED objective AAA 3rd and 2nd Divns. will complete capture of GREEN objective AAA It is imperative that FURENVILLE be captured as early as possible AAA Gds Divn. will be prepared to relieve or pass through 3rd and 2nd Divn. on the Corps Front to-night and will continue to attack at Dawn tomorrow objective WAMBAIX and the Rly. running north to H 2 central AAA Zero hour will be selected by G.O.C. Gds Divn. AAA 4th Corps have been ordered to protect right flank of Gds Divn.

From	6th Corps		
Place			
Time	1422		

MESSAGES AND SIGNALS. Army Form C. 2121.

DIARY

TO 2nd Divn.

Sender's Number: JD649
Day of Month: 8
AAA

Troops of Oxford Hussars will join squadron from 2nd Divn. to-morrow 9th rationed for consumption 10th AAA Strength 20 AAA Addressed 6th CTMT Coy. rptd 2nd Div. and Oxford Hussars.

From: 6th Corps
Time: 1530

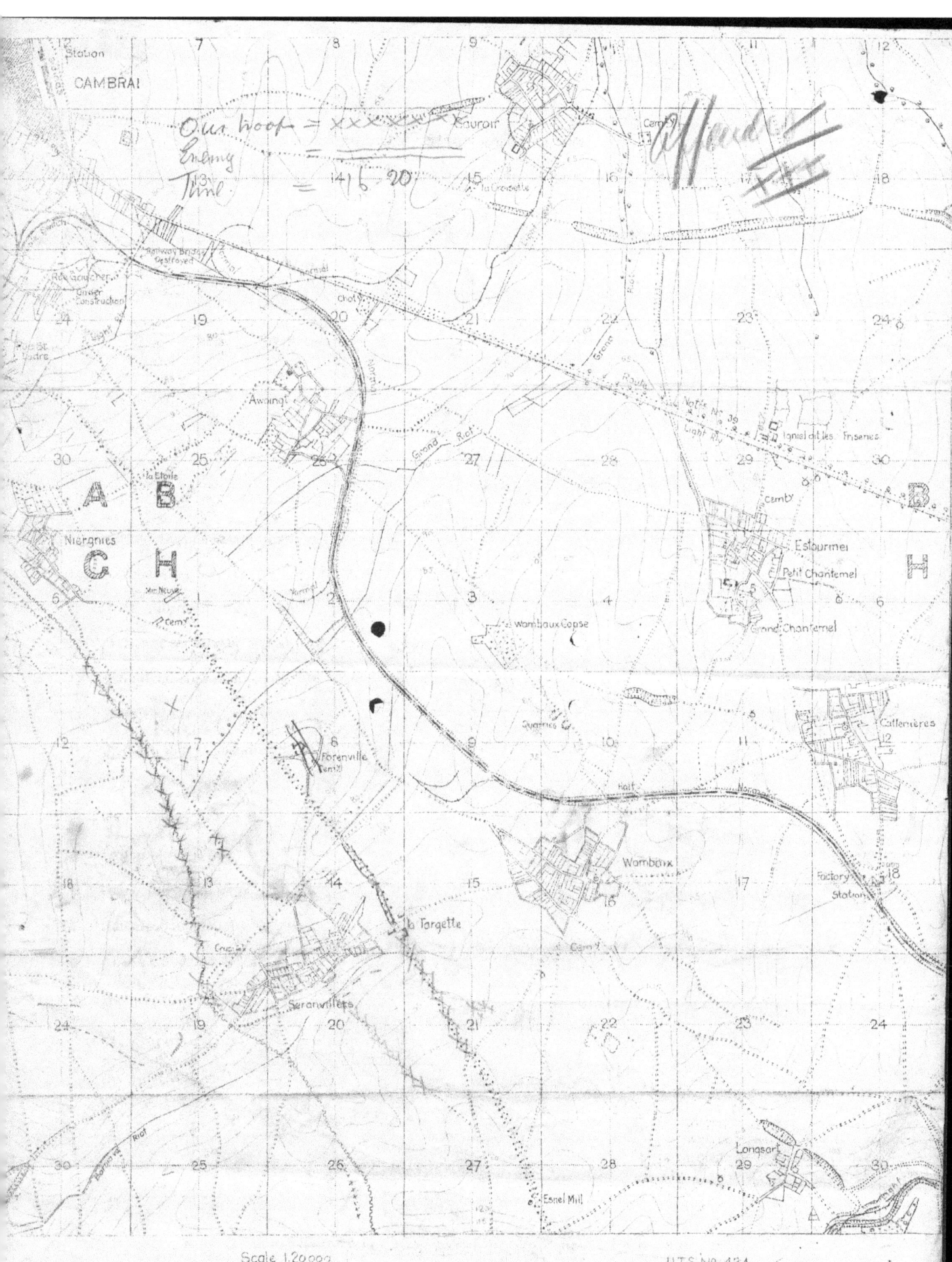

MESSAGE FORM

To _____   No _____

1. I am at _____
2. My line runs _____
3. My Platoon/Company is at _____ and is consolidating
4. My Platoon/Company is at _____ and has consolidated
5. Am held up by (a) M.G. (b) Wire at _____ (State where you are)
6. Enemy holding strong point _____
7. I am in touch with _____ on Right/Left at
8. I am not in touch with _____ on Right/Left
9. Am shelled from _____
10. Am in need of _____

11. Counter-attack forming at _____
12. Hostile (a) Battery (b) Machine Gun (c) Trench Mortar active at _____
13. Reinforcements wanted at _____
14. I estimate my present strength at _____ Rifles
15. Have captured _____
16. Prisoners belong to _____
17. Add any other useful information here. _____

Time _____ m   Name _____
Date _____ 1918.   Platoon _____
                Company _____
                Battalion _____

(A) Carry no maps or papers which may be of value to the Enemy.

(B) Give no information if captured, except the following which you are bound to give Name and Rank.

(C) Collect all captured maps and papers and send them in at once.

Margin note (handwritten): 16.30 Our line is held late in H14 C in H8b & H14 a C in H8b. Enemy should not now attempt in H14 b & d another Cemetery in H8c. J.G. Macdougall

Stamped: 755A

"A" Form.
MESSAGES AND SIGNALS.

Army Form C. 2121.

TO 2nd Divn.

Sender's Number.	Day of Month.	In reply to Number.	AAA
G200	8		

Ref. para 8 6th Corps order 388 dated 6th Oct. AAA 62nd Div. (Less H.Q.) will move forthwith to the support area AAA This area is now being cleared by G.Ds.Divn AAA 8th Inf. Bde. 3rd Divn. is now marching West through the area and will be clear of HAVRINCOURT by 6.30 pm AAA 3rd and 2nd Divns. will move back into right and left Divl. reserve areas respectively after relief by G.Ds. Divn. is complete or after Gds Divn. has passed through the front AAA H.Q. 62nd Divn. and 3rd Divns will change quarters at a time to be settled between the Divns concerned. AAA ACKNOWLEDGE.

From 6th Corps
Place
Time 1650 hrs.

"A" Form
MESSAGES AND SIGNALS.

Army Form C. 2121
(In pads of 100.)

This message is on a/c of:
DIARY

TO	2nd Divn.

Sender's Number.	Day of Month.	In reply to Number.	AAA
*G217	8		

You can now withdraw your troops through whom 17th Corps have passed.

From: 6th Corps
Time: 1945

"A" Form
MESSAGES AND SIGNALS.
Army Form C. 2121
(In pads of 100.)

DIARY

TO: 2nd Div.

Sender's Number.	Day of Month.	In reply to Number.	
G206	8		AAA

Ref.6th Corps G202 dated 8th Oct. AAA
Any troops of 3rd and 2nd Divn. on or East
of the LA TARGETTE - CAMBRAI Road will be
withdrawn to a line 300 yards W.of that
road on the 6th Corps front by 0500 Oct.
9th to enable Gds Div. to put down initial
barrage along that road AAA ACKNOWLEDGE.

From: 6th Corps
Place Time: 2000 hrs.

(Z)

"A" Form
MESSAGES AND SIGNALS.

Army Form C. 2121 (in pads of 100.)

Appendix XXIV
DIARY

TO	99th Bde	24th Div.
	M.G.Bn.	3rd Div.
	Gds Div.	6th Corps

Sender's Number.	Day of Month.	In reply to Number.	
G405	8		AAA

2nd Guards Brigade is taking over from 99th Brigade tonight and is renewing the attack at 0520 on October 9th AAA At 0520 barrage will come down on ESNES-CAMBRAI ROAD AAA 2nd Guards Bde forms up 300 yards West of Road AAA By 0445 all troops of 2nd Division will be withdrawn 300 yds West of Road FORENVILLE being evacuated AAA Troops of 2nd Division will be considered as relieved when troops of 2nd Guards Brigade have passed through AAA ACKNOWLEDGE AAA Addressed 99th Inf. Bde. M.G.Bn. repeated Guards Div. 24th Div. 3rd Div. 6th Corps.

From: 2nd Div.
Place:
Time: 2210

(Z) (Sd.) E.R.Clayton
Lt. Col.

"A" Form.
MESSAGES AND SIGNALS.

Army Form C. 2121.
(In pads of 100.)

5th 6th	99th Bdes	D.A.P.M.	Gds.Div.
D.C.L.I.	M.G.Bn.	3rd Div.	6th Corps
~~C.R.A.~~	~~Signals~~	~~62nd Div.~~	~~Q.~~
C.R.E	A.D.M.S.	63rd Div.	Train.

Sender's Number: G406
Day of Month: 8
AAA

On Oct.9th ~~Bdes.~~ and M.G.Bn. will move to areas allotted in 2nd Divn. E.133. issued on Oct 7th AAA ~~5~~ Bde will be clear of NOYELLES by 0830 AAA 6th Bde. less 17th R.Fusiliers will be clear of NOYELLES by 0930 AAA 99th Bde. and 17th R.Fusiliers will move as convenient AAA M.G.Bn. will move under orders of O.C.Battn. AAA Field Coys R.E. will remain in present area AAA Pioneers will move into area to be allotted by 2nd Divn. "Q" AAA "Q" are issuing instructions regarding move of Mob.Vet. Sec. Train and S.A.A. Section AAA Field Ambulances will be relieved under arrangements to be made by A.D.M.S. AAA Div. Headquarters close at L.13.c.2.3. and re-open at J.10.a. at 1000 AAA Units of 2nd Div. to acknowledge.

From: 2nd Divn.
Time: 2240
(Sd.) P.J.Mackesey.
Major for Lt.Col.

APPENDIX XXXVI

"A" Form
MESSAGES AND SIGNALS.

Army Form C. 2121
(in pads of 100.)

COPY

This message is on a/c of:
WAR DIARY APPENDIX

TO: 2nd Divn

Sender's Number: H 198
Day of Month: 9
AAA

6th Corps Artillery Instructions AAA 84th Bde R.G.A. less 9.2inch How Batty will be attcahed to Guards Divn AAA Remainder Heavy Artillery will be moved under orders B.G.H.A. as follows 63rd Bde to be affiliated to Guards Divn 58th Bty to support leading Divn 39th and 60th Bdes less 9.2 inch Batteries ready to support Guards Divn if required in Reserve 88th Bde AAA All 9.2 inch How Batteries will be parked between roads on L.22.a. W of MARCOING and along either side MARCOING NOYELLES Rd under orders B.G.H.A. AAA Field Arty AAA Brigades of 2nd and 3rd Divns will come under orders of their own Divns but will not be moved West of Line MARCOING NOYELLES AAA 14th and 76th Army Bdes will be in Corps Reserve and will move into wagon line areas at earliest opportunity as follows 14th R.H.A. Bde G.26.a or c 76th Bde G.26.b or d South of Canal AAA ACKNOWLEDGE AAA Addssd List B plus RA 3rd Army RA 4th and 17th Corps C.B.S.O. 14 and 76th Bdes F Corps M.T. Col 12 KB Coy 19 Obser Group.

From: 6th Corps
Time: 1215 hours

"A" Form
MESSAGES AND SIGNALS.
Army Form C. 2121
(In pads of 100.)

COPY

This message is on a/c of:
WAR DIARY APPENDIX

TO	C.R.E. 10/D.C.L.I.	
	C.E. VI Corps	"Q"

Sender's Number.	Day of Month.	In reply to Number.	AAA
G 16	9		

Commencing to-morrow 10th inst following work will be carried out under C.R.E. under direction of C.E. 6th Corps AAA By three Fd coys reconstruction of bridge in NOYELLES and maintenance of bridges between Grid S of L.17 L.18 and Grid between F and L squares AAA By 10/D.C.L.I maintenance of approaches to above bridges and of following roads E of Canal (a) NOYELLES RUMILLY (inclusive)
(b) NOYELLES MARCOING (exclusive) from Canal L.6.c. through L.18.central to Canal L.23.b.
(c) RUMILLY G.10.a. -) Corps Boundary A.28.c.90
(d) RUMILLY A.27.d.2.0 (e) Communications in RUMILLY AAA C.E. 6th Corps will communicate further details AAA Addssd C.R.E. and 10/D.C.L.I. to acknowlwdge repeated C.E. 6th Corps and "Q"

From 2nd Divn
Place
Time 2235

(sd) J.MACKESY Major

SECRET.

LOCATIONS 2ND DIVISION.

10th October, 1918.

2nd Division H.Q.	J.10.a.3.1.
2nd Signal Coy.	-do-
C.R.A.	J.10.b.1.9.
36th Bde. R.F.A.	Mt.SUR L'OEUVRE G.9.b.0.0.
41st Bde. R.F.A.	G.10.c.7.0.
C.R.E.	L.13.d.4.2.
5th Field Coy.	F.25.d.0.2.
226th Field Coy.	L.13.d.1.7.
483rd Field Coy.	L.14.a.3.5.
5th Inf. Brigade.	K.7.c.2.6.
24th R. Fusiliers	K.7.c.3.6.
2nd Oxf. & Bucks L.I.	K.8.central.
2nd H.L.I.	K.7.d.8.8.
6th Inf. Brigade.	K.7.d.3.0.
17th R. Fusiliers	K.9.d.1.0.
1st Kings Regt.	K.9.c.6.0.
2nd S. Staffs. Regt.	K.9.b.6.8.
99th Inf. Brigade.	L.13.c.1.3.
23rd R. Fusiliers	K.17.b.5.1.
1st R. Berks.	K.12.c.9.7.
1st K.R.R.C.	K.18.b.6.3.
M.G. Battalion	J.11.d.9.3.
10th D.C.L.I.(Pioneers)	L.13.c.4.3.
A.D.M.S.	J.10.a.3.1.

W. L. Taggart, Capt
for Lieut-Colonel,
General Staff, 2nd Division.

9th October, 1918.

LOCATIONS 2ND DIVISION - 11TH OCTOBER 1918.

Reference Map Sheet 57c and b 1/40,000.

APPENDIX XL

2nd Division H.Q.	J.10.a.3.1.
2nd Signal Coy.	- do -
C.R.A.	J.10.b.1.9.
36th Bde. R.F.A.	L.16.d.5.0.
41st Bde. R.F.A.	L.11.b.5.8.
C.R.E.	L.13.d.4.2.
5th Field Coy.	F.25.d.0.2.
226th Field Coy.	L.13.d.1.7.
483rd Field Coy.	L.14.a.3.5.
5th Infantry Brigade	K.7.c.2.8.
24th Roy. Fusiliers	K.7.c.3.6.
2nd Oxf. & Bucks L.I.	K.8.central
2nd H.L.I.	K.7.d.8.8.
6th Infantry Brigade	K.7.d.3.0.
17th Roy. Fusiliers	K.15.a.6.8.
1st King's Regt.	K.15.a.4.8.
2nd S. Staffs. Regt.	K.9.b.5.1.
99th Infantry Brigade	L.13.c.1.3.
23rd Roy. Fusiliers	K.17.b.5.1.
1st R. Berks. Regt.	K.12.c.9.7.
1st K.R.R.C.	K.17.b.5.1.
M.G. Battalion	J.11.d.9.3.
10th D.C.L.I. (Pioneers)	G.15.a.4.5.
A.D.M.S.	J.10.a.3.1.
5th Field Amb. (closed)	K.15.b.5.3.
6th Field Amb. (closed)	K.7.c.2.6.
100th Field Amb. (Div. Rest Stn.)	J.13.b.2.1.
D.A.D.O.S.	DOIGNIES
VI Corps H.Q.	HERMIES

W.I. Taggart
Captain
For Lieut-Colonel
General Staff - 2nd Division

APPENDIX XL (A)   2nd Division No.
                  G.S.948/17.

5th Inf. Bde.
6th Inf. Bde.
99th Inf. Bde.
C.R.A.
2/M.G. Battn.

The following points will be brought up at the
Divisional Conference to be held
on October 12th.

1. Infantry formations in the attack over open country.

2. In some of the recent operations it appears that the men have not used their rifles as much as they might have. One reason for this may be that bayonets are usually fixed at the beginning of an attack, and the rifle with a fixed bayonet is a clumsy weapon to fire with. Possibly if bayonets were not fixed at the beginning of an attack over open country the men would use their rifles much more than they do at present.

3. The action of forward Sections of Artillery acting in close liaison with Battn. Commanders.

4. On what occasions have Trench Mortars been used during recent operations?

5. Have there been any instances of prisoners after having been captured and sent to the rear, taking up weapons again and firing into our men? If so more careful arrangements must be made to collect prisoners in rear of the fighting line.

6. Any points which a Brigadier or C.D. may wish to bring forward.

                                (Sgd.) E.R. CLAYTON.
                                        Lieut Colonel.
11/10/18.   General Staff, 2nd Division.

2nd Division No. G.S. 948/17/1.

5th Inf. Brigade
6th Inf. Brigade
99th Inf. Brigade
C.R.A.
M.G. Battalion
10th D.C.L.I.

APPENDIX XL (B)

The following points were discussed at the Divisional Conference held on October 12th.

1. In the early stages of an advance it is usually best to adopt a diamond formation for Platoons of a Company or sections of a platoon instead of line. The advantages of this formation are that if the troops suddenly come under enfilade Machine Gun fire, the casualties are lighter than if moving in line, while the formation is one which readily admits of deployment.

    In the later stages of the attack when actually attacking the objective, line must be formed. Section and Platoon Commanders must then be prepared to advance by rushes. This must be practiced during training. It is probable if advances are made by rushes that quicker progress will be made than is usually the case at the present time.

    There is a danger which must be carefully guarded against of the supporting sections or platoons of a "diamond" formation getting drawn in with the leading troops. When this occurs the attack ceases to have any depth, and the result is that there is no possibility of the Company Commander influencing the fight by means of his reserves. This is very liable to happen where slow barrages are employed as is often unavoidable under present conditions.

2. There is no doubt that the men do not rely on their rifles as much as they should. The reason for this is probably to be found in the custom which has grown up since the early trench attacks of always attacking with fixed bayonets. These early attacks were often little more than bayonet charges. What we have to deal with now is a long advance which will ultimately lead up to the assault.

    Previous to the war we were trained to fix bayonets when getting to within 250 or 350 yards of the enemy's position. We should do the same now. We should start (except at night) without the fixed bayonet, and fix the bayonet on

P.T.O.

- 2 -

approaching the enemy. The men will thereby learn to use their rifles. If this is not done, the only logical method appears to be for the bayonet always to be fixed. The men will then become accustomed to the extra weight.

The G.O.C. does not wish to lay down what is to be done but leaves it to Brigadiers to see that means are taken for increasing fire during the attack.

3. With regard to the working of Artillery with Infantry Battalions, there are not enough Artillery Officers to make it possible to send a Liaison Officer with the Battalion Commander. The best course will be for the Battalion Commander to send an Observer for liaison purposes to the Battery or Section or F.O.O. whose duty it will be to come back to the Battalion Commander as necessary.

4. The C.R.A. pointed out the difficulty caused in ammunition supply by the employment of long slow barrages. 350 rounds per gun were fired in one barrage on October 8th.

5. Stokes have been used with good effect during recent operations.

6. The necessity of detailing a guard, however small, for prisoners and of not letting them wander about as they like, was emphasised.

E R Clayton
Lieut-Colonel,
General Staff, 2nd Division.

13th October, 1918.

APPENDIX XLI Diary

SECRET.
Copy No. 21

2nd Division Order No. 363.   12th October, 1918.

1. The Division (less Artillery, Field Coys. R.E. and Pioneer Battalion) will move to the SERANVILLERS Area on October 13th.

2. Details of moves are shown on attached March Table, which gives the routes to be followed if cross country tracks are impassable.
   If possible cross country tracks are to be used provided the times to pass points noted in the March Table are adhered to.

3. All troops will be East of the ST. QUENTIN CANAL by 1200.

4. Particular care is to be taken that roads are kept clear at halts.

5. The following distances will be kept :-
   200yds. between Battalions and their transport.
   200yds. between Battalions, Machine Gun Companies, Companies of Train and other units.

6. Divisional Headquarters will close at J.10.a. at 0930 and will open at SERANVILLERS at the same hour.

7. ACKNOWLEDGE.

E R Clayton
Lieut-Colonel,
General Staff, 2nd Division.

Issued at 1930 to :-

```
Copy No. 1  to  5th Inf. Brigade
         2      6th Inf. Brigade
         3      99th Inf. Brigade
         4      No. 2 M.G. Battalion
         5      C.R.A.
         6      C.R.E.
         7      2nd Signal Co.
         8      10th D.C.L.I.
         9      2nd Divisional Train
        10      Guards Division
        11      3rd Division
        12      62nd Division
        13      VI Corps
        14      "Q" 2nd Division
        15      A.D.M.S.
        16      2nd Division Gas Officer
        17      Camp Commandant
        18      D.A.P.M.
        19      D.A.D.V.S.
        20      D.A.D.O.S.
     21 - 25    G.S. Records.
```

March Table to accompany 2nd Division Order No.363.

Serial No.	Date	Unit.	From	To	Route.	Remarks.
1	October 13th	6th Inf. Bde.	Area K.9, K.10	NIERGNIES Area.	FLESQUIERES Cross roads L&b Cross roads l9.d	To pass FLESQUIERES at 0800. Cross canal by bridge at L.6.o. To be clear of Canal by 1045.
2	13th	5th Field Amb. and Bearer Divn. 100th Field Amb.	K.15.b.5.3	RUMILLY	NOYELLES – RUMILLY.	Moving under orders of G.O.C. 5th Inf. Bde. to RUMILLY. To be clear of Canal by 1055
3	13th	5th Inf. Bde.	Area K.7, K.8	RUMILLY.	FLESQUIERES – Cross roads L.8.b, – L.9.d – NOYELLES – RUMILLY	To pass FLESQUIERES at 0840. Cross canal by bridge at L.6.o. To be clear of Canal by 1125.
4	13th	6th Field Amb.	K.7.c.2.8	NIERGNIES		Moving under orders of G.O.C. 5th Bde. To be clear of canal bridge by 1130
5	13th	No.2 M.G.Bn.	J.11.d	RUMILLY	HERMIES – HAVRINCOURT – FLESQUIERES – cross roads L.8.b – cross roads L.9.d – NOYELLES – RUMILLY.	To pass FLESQUIERES at 0950. Cross canal bridge at L.6.o. To be clear of bridge L.6.o by 1200. To follow 6th Field Amb.
6	13th	99th Inf. Bde.	FLESQUIERES Area	WAMBAIX Area.	RIECOURT – MARCOING – MASNIERES – CREVECOEUR – WAMBAIX	To be clear of FLESQUIERES by 0750.

- 2 -

Serial No.	Date	Unit.	From	To	Route	Remarks.
7	13th	H.Q. Train No.2 Coy. No.3 Coy. No.4 Coy.	J.18.b. K.21.central J.36.b J.36.a	Area G.7 and 13.	HAVRINCOURT - RIBECOURT - MARCOING - Bridge L.12.o.	Following in rear of 99th Inf. Bde. as far as MARCOING. To be clear of bridge L.12.o by 1125.
8	13th	Mob. Vet. Sect.	J.15.b	Area G.7	HERMIES then as for serial No.7.	To be clear of Canal by 1130.
9	13th	S.A.A.Sect.	K.23.b	Area G.8	HAVRINCOURT - RIBECOURT - MARCOING - Canal bridge L.12.o.	To pass cross roads HAVRINCOURT K.27.b.9.2 at 0915 to be clear of canal by 1200.
10	13th	2/Signal Coy.	J.10.a	SERAN-VILLERS	HERMIES - RIBECOURT - CREVECOEUR.	To follow S.A.A. Sect. as far as MARCOING (Serial No.9)

Army Form W.3816.
1918.

'G' Diary

APPENDIX XLII

STRENGTH RETURN MADE UP TO 12 NOON SATURDAY 19th October 1918.

3rd Corps / Division.

UNIT.	(i.) Strength for previous week, compiled in accordance with A.G.'s instructions.		(ii.) Increase during week, due to drafts, etc., taken on strength of Unit.		(iii.) Totals from (i.) and (ii.)		(iv.) Decrease during week, casualties, etc., deducted from strength of Unit.		"A" Strength, excluding Attached.		"B" Not present with the Unit and not at the disposal of C.O. Included in column "A".		"A minus B." Available Fighting Strength, including Personnel of Battalion Transport and Quartermaster's Stores.		REMARKS. (Brief notes regarding (ii), (iv), and "B", etc.)
	Officers.	O.R.	Officers.	O.R.	Officers.	O.R.	Officers.	O.R.	Officers.	O.R.	Officers.	O.R.	Officers.	O.R.	
8th INFANTRY BRIGADE.															
2nd Royal Fusiliers.	40	755	1	34	41	789	1	30	40	759	9	152	31	607	
2nd Ox. & Bucks L.I.	54	738	5	56	59	794	1	33	58	761	7	110	58	651	
8th Highland L.I.	21	691	9	11	35	702	1	34	33	668	4	110	29	578	
Total Brigade.	118	2184	9	101	119	2285	3	97	111	2188	20	403	91	1770	
9th INFANTRY BRIGADE.															
17th Royal Fusiliers.	28	680	3	27	31	687	4	42	29	645	8	108	24	538	
1st King's Regiment.	50	806	1	20	51	825	2	28	49	797	8	117	41	680	
2nd Staff's Regt.	34	780	9	72	45	852	0	80	38	772	13	100	31	672	
Total Brigade.	112	2267	13	126	125	2393	15	197	116	2196	29	324	97	1873	
76th INFANTRY BRIGADE.															
2nd Royal Fusiliers.	34	739	3	67	37	806	2	96	35	709	8	115	27	594	
1st Royal Warks Regt.	50	768	8	22	48	820	8	135	38	675	8	135	27	540	
1st K.R. Rifle Corps.	53	733	9	19	57	797	0	111	55	643	11	115	34	528	
Total Brigade.	118	2175	16	108	152	2283	10	332	121	2091	27	365	88	1642	
Pioneer Battalion.															
18th D.C.L.I.	33	808	-	4	33	810	1	6	32	806	6	73	26	733	
3rd DIVISION.	584	7676	35	152	571	7763	25	862	545	7214	93	1184	80	6000	
No.3 Bn. L.C.Corps.	49	823	4	41	40	834	3	56	46	858	5	99	41	755	

Major General Commanding 3rd Division.

[P.T.O.]

CHANGES IN NOMINAL ROLLS OF OFFICERS.

(*i.e.*, Explanation of Increases and Decreases.)

Unit.	Joined.	Struck Off.	Cause.
99th INFANTRY BRIGADE.			
22nd Royal Fusiliers.			
2/Lt. A.G. RICHARD.			Reinforcement.
2/Lt. U.A. HARDY.		24-9-18.	To England sick, 19-9-18. (Auth: D.A.G. List No. 1912 dated 24-9-18)
2nd Oxf. & Bucks L.I.			
Lt. A.H. HUNT.)			
Lt. R.C.A. HYDER.)			
2/Lt. E.J. DEANE.)	7-10-18.		Reinforcements.
2/Lt. A.R. PRICE.)			
2/Lt. F.H. HUDSON.)			
2nd Highland L.I.			
2/Lt. J.H. HENRY.)	7-10-18.		Reinforcements.
2/Lt. R. MORRIS.)			
Major G.A.S. PARSONS, M.C.		8-10-18.	Transferred to 1/8th R.C.Bn., 8th Oct.1918. (Auth: AG/3198/9410(C) dated 10-9-18)
6th INFANTRY BRIGADE.			
17th Royal Fusiliers.			
Major S.J.H. HILL.	8-10-18.		From Senior Officers' Course, ALDERSHOT.
2/Lt. J. ELLIS.	4-10-18.		Reinforcement.
2/Lt. H.S. IRELAND.	4-10-18.		Do.
Major P.E.S.F. SMITH.		10-10-18.	Posted to 2/S.Staffs R, 10-10-18.
2/Lt. J.L. WEBB.		8-10-18.	Wounded.
2/Lt. A.P. POWELL.		8-10-18.	Do.
2/Lt. A.A. GREER.		8-10-18.	Do.
1st King's Regiment.			
2/Lt. J. BRAY.	8-10-18.		Reinforcement.
Lt. D. DOUARTY, M.C.		8-10-18.	Killed.
Capt. J.A. ANDERSON.		7-10-18.	Leave extended Medical Board. (Auth: VI Corps A/3/10 dated 7-10-18)
2nd S.Staffs Regt.			
Major P.E.S.F. SMITH.	10-10-18.		From 17th Royal Fus.
Lt. W.L. SMITH.)			
2/Lt. E.F. GREEN.)			
2/Lt. G.J. BRADBURY.)			
Lt. H.G. HILL.)	4-10-18.		Reinforcements.
Capt. H. GORDON.)			
2/Lt. A. HARDING.)			
2/Lt. A. MILLER.)			
2/Lt. S.H. BLAKING.	9-10-18.		Reinforcement.
Capt. E.A.V. SMITH.)			
Lt. R.A. KENDALL.)			
Lt. H. PARKER, M.C.)		11-10-18.	Posted to 1/6th S.Staff Regt. (Auth: AG/3198 6731(C) dated 9-10-18
Lt. M. WEBSTER.)			
Lt. E.J. TURNER)			
Lt. G.B. HAY.)			
2/Lt. H.L. BLOOMER.		8-10-18.	Wounded.
2/Lt. E.T. O'BRYAN.		4-10-18.	Do.
2/Lt. A.V. JONES.		9-10-18.	To England sick 27-9-. (Auth: D.A.G.List No. 1970 dated 9-10-18)

Contd........

LOCATIONS 2nd DIVISION - 14th October, 1918.

Reference Map - Sheet 57 C & b 1/40,000

Sheet:
57c   2nd Division H.Q.   SERANVILLERS   H.20.c.2.8.
 "   2nd Signal Coy. R.E.   - do -   - do -
 "   C.R.A.   - do -   - do -
57c   36th Bde R.F.A.   L.16.d.5.0.
 "   41st Bde R.F.A.   L.11.b.5.8.
 "   2nd D.A.C.   L.10.d.8.3.

57c   C.R.E.   H.14.a.5.2.
57c   5th Field Coy R.E.   F.25.d.0.2.
 "   226th Field Coy R.E.   L.13.d.1.7.
 "   483rd Field Coy R.E.   L.14.a.3.5.

57b   5th Inf. Brigade   G.15.b.3.6.
 "   24th Royal Fusiliers   G.21.a.9.5.
 "   2nd Oxf.& Bucks L.I.   G.15.d.2.7.
 "   2nd H.L.I.   G.15.a.9.1.
 "   5th L.T.M. Batty.   G.15.b.3.7.

 "   6th Inf. Brigade   A.30.c.0.0.
 "   17th Royal Fusiliers   A.30.c.5.4.
 "   1st King's Regt.   G.6.a.8.4.
 "   2nd South Staffs. Regt.   G.6.a.50.99.
 "   6th L.T.M.Batty.   G.5.a.4.9.

 "   99th Inf. Brigade   H.15.b.9.0.
 "   23rd Royal Fusiliers   H.16.a.8.5.
 "   1st Royal Berks Regt.   H.16.a.8.2.
 "   1st K.R.Rif. C.   H.16.a.5.1.
 "   99th L.T.M. Batty.   H.15.b.85.00.

 "   2nd M.G. Battn.   RUMILLY   G.16.c.6.8.

 "   10th D.C.L.I. (Pioneers)   G.15.a.4.5.

 "   A.D.M.S.   H.20.a.2.8.
 "   5th Field Ambulance   RUMILLY   (Closed)
 "   6th Field Ambulance   NIERGNIES   (Closed)
 "   100th Field Ambulance   RUMILLY   (Div. Rest Station)

 "   D.A.D.O.S.   LA TARGETTE
 "   D.A.P.M.   SERANVILLERS   H.19.b.9.8.

       VI Corps H.Q.   GRAND CHANTEMEL H.5.central
       Guards Division   BOUSSIERES   C.20.b.8.6.
       3rd Division   FLESQUIERES   K.24.b.3.7.
       62nd Division   PETIT CHANTEMEL H.5.b.5.5.

APPENDIX
XLIII

Capt.,
for Lieut. Col
G.S, 2nd Divn.

APPENDIX XLIV

LOCATIONS 2nd DIVISION 15th October 1918
Reference Map Sheet 57 c and b 1/40000

Sheet			
57b	2nd Division H.Q.	SERANVILLERS	H.20.a.2.8
"	2nd Signal Co	-do-	-do-
"	C.R.A.	-do-	H.20.a.4.7
57c	36th Bde R.F.A.	L.16.d.5.0.	
"	41st Bde. R.F.A.	L.11.b.5.6	
"	2nd D.A.C.	L.10.d.8.3.	
57b	C.R.E.	H.14.c.5.2.	
57c	5th Field Coy. R.E.	F.25.d.0.2.	
"	226 Field Coy. R.E.	L.13.d.1.7.	
"	483rd Field Coy. R.E.	L.14.a.3.5.	
b	5th Inf. Bde.	G.15.b.3.6.	
"	24th R. Fusiliers	G.21.a.9.5.	
"	2nd Ox. & Bucks L.I.	G.15.d.2.7.	
"	2nd H.L.I.	G.15.a.9.1.	
"	5th L.T.M. Battery	G.15.b.3.7.	
"	6th Inf. Bde.	A.30.c.0.0.	
"	17th R. Fusiliers	A.30.c.5.4.	
"	1st King's Regt.	G.6.a.8.4.	
"	2nd S. Staffs.	G.6.a.50.99	
"	6th L.T.M. Battery	G.5.a.4.9.	
"	99th Inf. Bde.	H.15.b.9.0.	
"	23rd R. Fusiliers	H.16.a.8.5.	
"	1st R. Berks.	H.16.a.8.2.	
"	1st K.R.R.C.	H.16.a.5.1.	
"	99th L.T.M. Battery	H.15.b.85.00.	
"	2nd M.G. Battn.	RUMILLY	G.15.c.6.8.
"	10th D.C.L.I.(Pnrs)	G.15.a.4.5.	
"	A.D.M.S.	SERANVILLERS	H.14.d.3.1.
"	5th Field Amb.	RUMILLY	G.15.a.6.0.
"	6th Field Amb.	FORENVILLE	H.8.c.6.9.
"	100th Field Amb.	NOYELLES (moving to WAMBAIX) (Div. Rest Station)	
"	D.A.D.O.S.	LA TARGETTE	
"	D.A.P.M.	SERANVILLERS	H.19.b.9.8.
"	VI Corps H.Q.	GRAND CHANTEMEL	H.5.central
"	Guards Division	BOUSSIERES	C.20.b.8.6.
"	3rd Division	FLESQUIERES	K.24.b.3.7.
"	62nd Division	PETIT CHANTEMEL	H.5.b.5.5.

B. H. Harrison
Captain
For Lieut-Colonel
General Staff - 2nd Division.

"A" Form.
MESSAGES AND SIGNALS.

APPENDIX XLV

TO	5" Bde	M.G. Battn	Q	Signals
	6" Bde	CRE	ADMS	
	99" Bde	CRA	APM	

Sender's Number.	Day of Month.	In reply to Number.	AAA
G.95	18		

5th Inf Bde 226 Field Coy R.E. One Company M.G. Battn and 5th Field Ambulance will be prepared to move October 19th to CARNIERES – BOUSSIERES area aaa details later aaa acknowledge.

From 2nd Div
Time 14.20

(Z) B H Hamilton Capt G.95

MESSAGES AND SIGNALS.

Army Form C. 2121.
(In pads of 100.)

PRIORITY
to 5th Bde
and M.G. Bn

APPENDIX XLVI

TO	5th Bde	6th Bde	99th Bde	C.R.A.	C.R.E.
	M.Gun Bn	D.C.L.I.	Signals	"Q"	ADMS DAPM
	Train Guards	3rd Divn	62nd Div	VI Corps	

Sender's Number.	Day of Month.	In reply to Number.	
G 98	18		AAA

5th Inf Bde one Coy M.G. Bn 226th Fd Coy and 5th Fd Ambce will march on October 19th to area BOUSSIERES-CARNIERES under orders of G.O.C. 5th Inf Bde AAA Not to enter BOUSSIERES CARNIERES before 1700 hours AAA No restrictions as to route AAA O.C. M.G. BN will inform 5th Inf Bde whch Coy is detailed repeating to this office AAA 100 yds distance between Inf Coys 200 yds between Battalions and their transport and 200 yds between all Units AAA Cross country tracks to be used as much as possible AAA 5th Bde H.Q. at CARNIERRES to take over H.Q. of 3rd Guards Brigade AAA 5th Inf Brigade M.Gun Bn A.D.M.S. C.R.E. to acknowledge.

From 2nd Div
Place
Time 1800

(sd) E.R. CLAYTON Lt Col

APPENDIX XLVII

SECRET

War Diary
Copy No. 16

2nd Division Order No. 364.

19th October 1918.

1. The advance of the Third Army is being continued on LE QUESNOY.

2. The first stage of the advance is the capture of the high ground East of the River SELLE.

3. The Guards and 62nd Divisions in conjunction with the IV Corps on the right and the XVII Corps on the left are attacking at 0200, October 20th.

4. The 42nd Division is on the left of the 17 Corps and the 19th Division on the right of the XVII Corps.

5. The attack is being carried out as a surprise with no preliminary bombardment.

6. The final objective of the VI Corps is the high ground West of ROMERIES and VERTAIN. This will be the main line of resistance of the Corps.

7. As soon as the final objective has been gained bridges will be at once constructed on the River SELLE in preparation for further advance.

8. All troops of the 2nd Division will be at 2 hours notice from 0700, October 20th.

9. ACKNOWLEDGE.

P.J. Mackesy Major
for Lieut-Colonel,
General Staff, 2nd Division.

Issued at 1015 to :-

Copy No. 1 to 5th Inf. Brigade
2   6th Inf. Brigade
3   99th Inf. Brigade
4   No. 2 M.G. Battalion
5   C.R.A.
6   C.R.E.
7   2nd Signal Co.
8   10th D.C.L.I.
9   2nd Divisional Train
10 "Q" 2nd Division
11 A.D.M.S.
12 D.A.P.M.
13 S.A.A. Section
14 - 18 G.S. Records.

COPY.   **APPENDIX XLVIII**

PRIORITY TO 10th D.C.L.I. & Train.

5th Bde   6th Bde   99th Bde   D.C.L.I.   Train
Q   C.RE.   A.D.M.S.   Signals   D.A.P.M.

G. 113   19

10th D.C.L.I. will move to ST HILAIRE tomorrow 20th inst. aaa To be clear of present billets by 0900 aaa No restrictions as to route aaa Addsd 10th D.CL.I. to ACKNOWLEDGE reptd. Bdes. C.RE. Signals, Train, Q, A.DMM.S., D.A.P.M..

2nd Divn.

1445

(Sgd.) P.J. MACKESY
Major G.S.

"A" Form.
MESSAGES AND SIGNALS.

Army Form C. 2121.
(In pads of 100.)

TO:
- 5th Bde, C.R.A. Train A.D.M.S.
- 6th Bde C.R.E. Q   D.A.P.M.
- 99th Bde Signals
- M.G. Batt 10th D.C.L.I.

Sender's Number: G.112
Day of Month: 19
AAA

The Division will be prepared to move forward on October 20th into close Billets as follows aaa 5th Inf. Bde Group from BOUSSIERES and CARNIERS to ST HILAIRE aaa 99th Inf. Bde. 483rd Field Coy. R.E. 100th Field Ambce. M.G. Battn less 1 Coy. to BOUSSIERES and CARNIERS aaa Separate orders are being issued for move of 10th D.C.L.I. aaa 6th Bde. Group to remain at NIERGNIES aaa If the above moves take place the nucleus of Inf. Battns will proceed to Reception Camp at NIERGNIES sufficient tentage being sent to Reception Camp for accommodation today aaa Movement XIII S.A.A. Sectn and Train will be arranged by 2nd Division Q aaa Divisional H.Q. will remain at SERANVILLERS   Brigades M.G. Battn. 10th D.C.L.I. C.R.E. to acknowledge

From: 2nd Divn.
Time: 1445 hrs

APPENDIX L

LOCATIONS 2ND DIVISION - 20TH OCTOBER 1918.

Reference Map Sheet 57c and b.1/40,000

Sheet			
57b	2nd Division H.Q.	SERANVILLERS	H.20.a.2.8.
"	2nd Signal Coy.	-do-	-do-
"	C.R.A.	-do-	H.20.a.4.7.
"	36th Bde. R.F.A.	V.25.c.6.0.	
"	41st Bde. R.F.A.	-do-	
"	2nd D.A.C.	B.29.d.8.6.	
"	C.R.E.	H.14.c.5.2.	
"	5th Field Coy. R.E.	H.8.c.6.7.	
"	226th Field Coy. R.E.	C.20.b.8.9.	
"	483rd Field Coy. R.E.	H.14.d.9.4.	
"	5th Inf. Bde.	C.13.d.0.5.	
"	24th R. Fusiliers	C.13.d.1.5.	
"	2nd Ox. & Bucks L.I.	C.13.c.5.3.	
"	2nd H.L.I.	BOUSSIERES	
"	5th L.T.M. Battery	C.21.a.5.2.	
"	6th Inf. Bde.	A.30.c.0.0.	
"	17th R. Fusiliers	A.30.c.5.4.	
"	1st King's Regt.	G.6.a.8.4.	
"	2nd S. Staffs.	G.6.a.50.99	
"	6th L.T.M. Battery	G.5.a.4.9.	
"	99th Inf. Bde.	H.15.b.9.0.	
"	23rd R. Fusiliers	H.16.a.8.5.	
"	1st R. Berks	H.16.a.8.2.	
"	1st K.R.R.C.	H.16.a.5.1.	
"	99th L.T.M. Battery	H.15.b.85.00	
"	2nd M.G. Battn.	RUMILLY	G.15.c.6.8.
"	10th D.C.L.I. (Pioneers)	G.15.a.4.5.	
"	A.D.M.S.	SERANVILLERS	H.14.d.3.1.
"	5th Field Amb.	C.13.c.5.5.	
"	6th Field Amb.	FORENVILLE	H.8.c.6.9.
"	100th Field Amb.	LA TARGETTE (Div. Rest Station)	
"	D.A.D.O.S.	LA TARGETTE	
"	D.A.P.M.	SERANVILLERS	H.19.b.9.8.
"	VI Corps H.Q.	GRAND CHANTEMEL	H.5.central
"	Guards Division	BOUSSIERES	C.20.b.8.6.
"	3rd Division	FLESQUIERES	K.24.b.3.7.
"	62nd Division	BEVILLERS	C.22.d.3.2.
"	S.A.A. Section	G.13.d.7.5.	

R. H. Harrison
Captain
For Lieut-Colonel
General Staff - 2nd Division.

CHANGES IN NOMINAL ROLLS OF OFFICERS.

(*i.e.*, Explanation of Increases and Decreases.)

Unit.	Joined.	Struck Off.	Cause.
5th INFANTRY BRIGADE.			
24th Royal Fusiliers.			
T/2nd Lt.G.E.F.S. CLEMENTS.		11-10-18.	To England for duty with R.A.F. (Auth: AG/2155/226(0) of 4-10-18.)
2nd Oxf.& Bucks L.I.			
2nd Lt.C.H.SHEPPARD.			
2/Lt. J. THORNE.			
2/Lt. F.G. BOBBY.			
Lt.F.C.L.A.LOWNDES.			
Lt.R.A.FITZ-GERALD.	18-10-18.		Reinforcements.
Lt.P.G.R.WHITEHEAD.			
Lt. H.A.VERNON.			
2/Lt.F.G.HOLLAND.			
Capt. A.J.CHAFFEY.			
2nd Highland L.I.			
2/Lt. J. STEEL.	10-10-18.		Reinforcements.
2/Lt.E.K.HUMPHREYS.			
6th INFANTRY BRIGADE.			
1st King's Regt.			
2/Lt. F.DENOVEN.	12-10-18		Reinforcement.
2/Lt. E. PECK.	17-10-18.		Do.
2nd S.Staffs Regt.			
2/Lt. H.JOHNSON.	18-10-18.		Reinforcement.
99th INFANTRY BRIGADE.			
1st Royal Berks Regt.			
Lt.Col.J.A.SOUTHEY.	16-10-18.		Reinforcement. (Auth: AG/2155/6686(0) of 13-10-18)
Lt.Col.D.W.POWELL, D.S.O.		18-10-18.	To England for six months tour of duty. (Auth: AG/2155/6784(0) of 10-10-18.)
2/Lt.T.A.DEAN, M.C.		18-10-18.	Taken on Est.99th T.M.B. vice Lt.G.W.OAKESHOTT, 1/K.R.R.C. trans. to R.A.F. (Auth: AG/2154/266(0) of 20-9-18).
1st K.R.Rifle Corps.			
A/Capt.F. HALL.	18-10-18.		Reinforcements.
2/Lt. T.H.WALLIS.			
Lt.P.G.SOMERVILLE.			To Rifle Brigade 14-10-18. (Auth: AG/2155/6211(0) of 21-9-18)
10th D.C.L.I.			
2/Lt. H.W. ALDRICH.		1-10-18.	Evacuated to England sick 1-10-18.
No.2 Bn. M.G.Corps.			
Lt. J.S. BOOTH.	18-10-18.		Reinforcements.
2/Lt.F.W.FENNELL.			
Lt. A.S. BECK.		13-10-18.	To U.K. for tour of duty. Auth:AG/6990(0) of 8-10-18.
2/Lt.S.J.W.TOWLER,DCM.			
2/Lt. S.D.MARSH.		13-10-18.	Evacuated sick.

Army Form W.3815.

APPENDIX L.A

"G" Diary

.... Corps. 2nd (Division). 1918.

STRENGTH RETURN MADE UP TO 12 NOON SATURDAY 12th October 1918.

UNIT.	(i.) Strength for previous week, compiled in accordance with A.G.'s instructions.		(ii.) Increase during week, due to drafts, etc., taken on strength of Unit.		(iii.) Totals from (i.) and (ii.)		(iv.) Decrease during week - casualties, etc., deducted from strength of Unit.		"A" Strength, excluding Attached.		"B" Not present with the Unit and not at the disposal of C.O. Included in column "A."		"A minus B." Available Fighting Strength, including Personnel of Battalion Transport and Quartermaster's Stores.		REMARKS. Brief notes regarding (ii.), (iv.), and "B", etc.
	Officers.	O.R.	Officers.	O.R.	Officers.	O.R.	Officers.	O.R.	Officers.	O.R.	Officers.	O.R.	Officers.	O.R.	
5th INFANTRY BRIGADE.															
24th Royal Fusiliers.	40	759	—	15	40	774	1	13	39	761	10	147	29	614	
2nd Oxf. & Bucks L.I.	39	756	9	44	48	800	—	13	48	787	8	127	40	660	
2nd Highland L.I.	32	686	3	212	34	898	—	3	34	895	6	116	28	779	
Total Brigade.	111	2201	11	271	122	2472	1	29	121	2443	24	390	97	2053	
6th INFANTRY BRIGADE.															
17th Royal Fusiliers.	32	638	—	17	32	655	—	16	32	639	9	110	23	529	
1st King's Regiment.	29	757	2	12	31	769	—	13	31	756	8	115	23	641	
2nd S.Staffs Regt.	34	783	1	29	35	812	—	5	35	807	14	121	21	686	
Total Brigade.	95	2178	3	58	98	2236	—	34	98	2202	31	346	67	1856	
99th INFANTRY BRIGADE.															
23rd Royal Fusiliers.	35	709	—	35	35	744	—	10	35	734	9	128	26	606	
1st Royal Berks Regt.	36	675	1	49	37	724	2	22	35	702	13	96	22	606	
1st K.R.Rifle Corps.	35	646	2	29	37	675	1	23	36	652	11	116	25	536	
Total Brigade.	106	2030	3	113	109	2143	3	55	106	2088	33	340	74	1748	
Pioneer Battalion.															
10th D.C.L.I.	31	805	—	7	31	812	1	17	30	795	7	98	23	697	
TOTAL DIVISION.	343	7214	17	449	360	7663	5	135	355	7528	94	1184	261	6344	
31.2 Bn. M.G.Corps.	46	862	2	43	48	905	3	10	45	895	7	81	38	814	

(Sgd) E Thompson
Major General,
Commanding 2nd Division.

[P.T.O.

C O P Y.   APPENDIX   LI

PRIORITY.
                    0647   0709

T O   2nd Divn.

G. 155   20   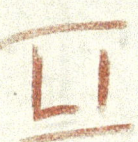 238

Reference 6th Corps warning order 394 para 1 2nd
and 3rd Divs. will move forward this morning to
area mentioned therin   aaa   No restrictions as to XX
time or route   aaa   G.O.Cs 2nd and 3rd Divs will
report to Corps Headquarters at 1000 hrs this morning
aaa   Ad sd. 2nd and 3rd Div. to acknowledge reptd
Gds. 62 Div Adv. 3 Army 3 Army Flank Corps Q A.DM.S.

                                    0718

     6th Corps

     0634

"A" Form.
MESSAGES AND SIGNALS.

Army Form C. 2121.

Priority to Bdes and M.G. Batt

APPENDIX LII

TO	5th Bde 6th Bde 99th Bde MG Batt CRA CRE Signals Train DCLI 3rd Div DAPM Guards 62nd Div 6th Corps ADMS "Q"

Sender's Number	Day of Month	In reply to Number	AAA
G 123	20		

On October 20th M.G. Battalion less 1 Coy will march at 0930 to CARNIERES - BOUSSIERES area route CREVECOEUR - WAMBAIX billets from 99th Bde. AAA 5th Inf. Bde. group now at BOUSSIERES and CARNIERES will move to ST HILAIRE to be East of BOUSSIERES by 1100 AAA 99th Brigade 483rd Field Co. 100th Field Ambulance will move to CARNIERES and BOUSSIERES area under orders of G.O.C. 99th Brigade to be clear of WAMBAIX by 1100 AAA Brigades and M.G. Batt to acknowledge

From: 2nd Division
Place:
Time: 0755

"A" Form.
MESSAGES AND SIGNALS.

Army Form C. 2121.

APPENDIX 11 A

TO: 2nd Divn.

Sender's Number: G.167.
Day of Month: 20
AAA

Ref. para 6 of 6th Corps Order No.395 dated 19th Oct. aaa Date postponed 24 hours aaa Acknowledge aaa Addsd recipients Order 395

From: Sixth Corps
Time: 1513

APPENDIX. LIII.

SECRET

LOCATIONS 2nd DIVISION – 21st October, 1918.

Reference Map Sheet 57g   1/40,000.

Sheet			
57b.	2nd Division H.Q.	SERANVILLERS	H.20.a.2.8.
"	2nd Signal Co.	-do-	-do-
"	C.R.A.	-do-	H.20.a.4.7.
"	36th Bde. R.F.A.	V.25.a.6.0.	
"	41st Bde. R.F.A.	-do-	
"	2nd D.A.C.	B.29.d.6.6.	
"	C.R.E.	H.14.c.5.2.	
"	5th Field Co. R.E.	H.8.c.6.7.	
"	226th Field Co. R.E.	V.25.c.7.8.	
"	483rd Field Co. R.E.	C.20.b.9.9.	
"	5th Inf. Brigade	C.6.b.9.2.	
"	24th R. Fusiliers	V.25.d.3.3.	
"	2nd Oxf. & Bucks L.I.	D.1.c.5.1.	
"	2nd H.L.I.	C.6.b.9.4.	
"	5th L.T.M. Battery	C.6.d.9.9.	
"	6th Inf. Brigade	A.30.c.0.0.	
"	17th R. Fusiliers	A.30.c.5.4.	
"	1st King's Regt.	G.6.a.8.4.	
"	2nd S. Staffs Regt.	G.6.a.50.99.	
"	6th L.T.M. Battery	G.5.a.4.9.	
"	99th Inf. Brigade	C.13.d.0.5.	
"	23rd R. Fusiliers	C.21.a.5.1.	
"	1st R. Berks	C.13.d.1.5.	
"	1st K.R.R.C.	C.13.c.55.25.	
"	99th L.T.M. Battery	C.13.c.9.0.	
"	No. 2 M.G. Battalion	C.20.b.9.5.	
"	10th D.C.L.I. (Pioneers)	V.25.d.20.45.	
"	A.D.M.S.	SERANVILLERS	H.14.d.3.1.
"	5th Field Ambulance	C.13.c.5.5.	
"	6th Field Ambulance	FORENVILLE	H.8.c.6.9.
"	100th Field Ambulance Bearers	LA TARGETTE (Div. Rest Station). C.13.d.0.0.	
"	D.A.D.O.S.	LA TARGETTE	
"	D.A.P.M.	SERANVILLERS	H.19.b.9.8.
"	VI Corps H.Q.	GRAND CHANTELMEL	H.5.central
"	Guards Division	BOUSSIERES	C.20.b.9.6.
"	3rd Division	FLESQUIERES	K.24.b.3.7.
"	62nd Division	BEVILLERS	C.22.d.3.2.
"	S.A.A. Section	BOUSSIERES	C.21.a.

B. H. Hamilton

Captain,
for Lieut-Colonel,
General Staff, 2nd Division.

"A" Form.
MESSAGES AND SIGNALS.

Army Form C. 2121.
(In pads of 100.)

Appendix. LIV

TO	C.R.E.
	10th D.C.L.I.
	"Q"

Sender's Number.	Day of Month.	In reply to Number.	
G.131.	20		AAA

From morning 21st 2nd Div. will be responsible for maintenance of ST VAAST – ST PYTHON road to River SELLE inclusive aaa 10th D.C.L.I. will work on this road aaa Details will be arranged by C.R.E. aaa Addd C.R.E. and 10th D.C.L.I. repeated "Q"

From: 2nd Div.
Place:
Time: 1410.

(Sgd) B. MACKESEY.
Major.

"A" Form.
MESSAGES AND SIGNALS.

Army Form C. 2121.
(In pads of 100.)

APPENDIX LV

PRIORITY to Bdes. M.G.Bn. D.C.L.I.

TO:
5th Bde.	C.R.E.	Train	D.A.P.M.
6th Bde.	D.C.L.I.	Guards Divn.	
99th Bde.	M.G. Bn.	"Q"	
C.R.A.	Signals	A.D.M.S.	

Sender's Number: G.243 — Day of Month: 21 — AAA

Moves to-morrow aaa 5th Bde. to line aaa H.Q. V.29.d.8.5. aaa To be clear of billets in ST. HILAIRE by 1800 aaa 99th Bde. aaa H.Q. to present 5th Bde. H.Q. C.6.b.9.2. aaa One Battalion to East of river SELLE aaa This Battalion to stage at ST VAAST arriving there by 1100 aaa 10th D.C.L.I. will give up half their accomodation from 1100 till 2359 22nd inst. to this Battalion aaa 2 Battalions and T.M.B. to ST HILAIRE aaa Not to enter ST HILAIRE before 1800 aaa Units in ST HILAIRE take over from 52nd L.I. (less Battalion H.Q.) H.L.I. 5th T.M.B. aaa 6th Bde. aaa H.Q. to present 52nd L.I. H.Q. D.I.c.5.1. aaa One Battalion to ST HILAIRE taking over from 2nd Battalion Coldstream Guards aaa 2 Battalions and T.M.B. to bivouac about C.11.b. aaa 6th Bde. march by AVOINGT - IGNIEL - CARNIERES - BOUSSIERES not to enter CARNIERES before 1430 to be clear by 1530 aaa Field Coys. will be located as arranged by C.R.E. aaa

"A" Form.
MESSAGES AND SIGNALS.

Army Form C. 2121.
(In pads of 100.)

M.G. Battn. less 2 Companies to ST. HILAIRE taking over from Guards M.G. Battn. aaa To leave BOUSSIERES at 1100 aaa 2 Companies to line under Battalion orders aaa Brigades D.C.L.I. M.G. Battn. to ACKNOWLEDGE.

From: 2nd Divn
Time: 2325

APPENDIX LVI [SECRET]

Copy No. 21........

2nd Division Order No. 365.   21st October, 1918.
_____

1.   The VI Corps is attacking on October 23rd in conjunction with the IV Corps on the right and XVII Corps on the left.

2.   The 2nd Division is advancing through the Guards Division. The 3rd Division on the right is advancing through the 62nd Division with the 8th Inf. Brigade on the left, 76th Inf. Brigade on the right, and 9th Inf. Brigade in Reserve. The 57th Brigade, 19th Division, at present holding the line on the left, is advancing on the left of the 2nd Division.

3.   The objectives of the 2nd Division are shewn on the map issued with this Order.

        First Objective   RED
        Second Objective   GREEN
        Third Objective   BROWN
        Objective for)
        24th October   )   BLUE

4.   The attack will be carried out by the 5th Inf. Brigade. The 99th Inf. Brigade will be in Support with 1 Battalion East of the river SELLE before ZERO. The 6th Inf. Brigade will be in Reserve.

5.   The troops detailed to attack VERTAIN and the RED Line from the Right Divisional Boundary to W.9.b.2.0. will form up about the road in W.19.a. and b. and advance in touch with troops of the 3rd Division.
      The troops detailed to attack the RED objective from W.9.b.2.0. to the Left Divisional Boundary will cross the HARPIES River at ZERO and forming up on the East bank will be ready to advance at ZERO plus 20.
      The objective will be in the first instance, the RED line from the road junction in W.3.d. to the Left Divisional Boundary. After the troops detailed to capture VERTAIN have reached the RED objective, both detachments will work inwards and effect a junction.

                                                            P.T.O.

- (2) -

6.   The 99th Inf. Brigade will be prepared to go through on to the BLUE line on October 24th.

7.   Five Brigades of Field Artillery are available on the Divisional Front for the attack on October 23rd. The Artillery arrangements will be as follows :-

(a) The attack on the first (RED) objective.

    (i) For the troops attacking VERTAIN a creeping barrage will come down at 0320 hrs. on the line W.20.central, W.20.a.2.7. This barrage will dwell on the opening line for 4 minutes and will then creep forward at 100 yds. in 6 minutes.

    (ii) For the attack on the remainder of the first (RED) objective from W.9.b.2.0. to the Left Divisional Boundary, the barrage will come down on a line 300 yds. East of the HARPIES River from W.9.c.7.4. to the Left Divisional Boundary at 0320 hrs. This barrage will dwell for 20 minutes and will then creep forward at 100 yds. in 3 minutes to the RED objective.
From ZERO onwards the roads forming the first objective and the sunken road in W.a. and c. will be bombarded in addition to other points which will be indicated to C.R.A. 2nd Division.

(b) For the attack on the second (GREEN) objective in conjunction with the 3rd Division a creeping barrage will come down at 0840 hrs. moving forward at 100 yds. in 3 minutes as far as the line Cross Roads W.4.b. to Divisional Boundary W.4.d.9.6. Forward of this line through the village of ESCARMAIN the barrage will move at 100 yds. in 6 minutes.

(c) For the attack on the final (BROWN) objective the barrage will be put down at 1212 hrs. on a line 300 yds. in front of the GREEN Line and will creep forward at 100 yds. in 4 minutes.
A detailed statement and Barrage Map will be issued later.

- (3) -

8. The O.C. Machine Gun Battalion will arrange to support the attack of the 5th Inf. Brigade.

9. One Troop Oxfordshire Hussars now attached to Guards Division for communication purposes will be attached to 2nd Division from October 23rd.
One Troop Oxfordshire Hussars and a detachment of cyclists are attached to the 2nd Division for tactical purposes.

10. Contact Aeroplanes will call for flares at 0700 hrs., 1000 hrs. and 1400 hrs.
A counter-attack plane will be in the air from daylight onwards.

11. Should the enemy withdraw the Infantry will not follow up beyond the BROWN Line.
Touch will be kept by means of Cavalry and Cyclists.

12. A detachment of Tunnellers now attached to Guards Division is being transferred to the 2nd Division on October 23rd. This detachment is to be employed in discovering and clearing booby traps.

13. O.C., Signals will send round a watch to Brigades and R.A. after 1500 hrs. on October 22nd for the purpose of synchronising the time.

14. Headquarters on October 23rd are as follows :-

      5th Inf. Brigade ... V.29.d.8.7.
      6th Inf. Brigade ... D.1.c.5.1.
      57th Inf. Brigade .. V.5.c.9.1.
      8th Inf. Brigade)
      76th Inf. Brigade) E.1.b.2.5. approx.

P.T.O.

-(4)-

15. Command of the Front will pass to G.O.C. 2nd Division at 0320 hrs. October 23rd.

16. Divisional Headquarters will close at SERANVILLERS at 1000 hrs. October 22nd and re-open at ST. HILAIRE at the same hour.

17. ACKNOWLEDGE.

E R Clayton
Lieut-Colonel,
General Staff, 2nd Division.

Issued at 2340 to :-

```
Copy No.  1  to   5th Inf. Brigade *
          2       6th Inf. Brigade *
          3       99th Inf. Brigade *
          4       No. 2 M.G. Battalion *
          5       C.R.A. *
          6       C.R.E. *
          7       2nd Signal Co. *
          8       10th D.C.L.I.
          9       Guards Division
         10       3rd Division
         11       19th Division
         12       62nd Division
         13       VI Corps
         14       84th H.A. Bde.
         15       "Q" 2nd Division *
         16       A.D.M.S. *
         17       Oxfordshire Hussars
         18-22    G.S. Records.
```

* Map issued.

SECRET A4(1) 22/10/18

FRANCE.
SHEET 51ᵃ S.E.
EDITION 3 a
Scale 1: 20,000
20,000
Trenches revised from information received to 12-10-18.

LEGEND
Corps Bdy
Divnl's line being relieved
Divisions
Approx present front line
First Objective
Second do
Final Objective for future operations

2nd Division
War Diaries
General Staff

October 1918

LOCATIONS 2nd DIVISION - 22nd October 1918.

Reference Map Sheet 57b, 1/40,000.

2nd Division H.Q.	SERANVILLERS	H.20.a.2.8.
2nd Signal Coy.	-do-	-do-
C.R.A.	SERANVILLERS	H.20.a.4.7.
36th Bde. R.F.A.	V.25.a.6.0.	
41st Bde. R.F.A.	..do..	
2nd D.A.C.	B.29.d.6.6.	
C.R.E.	H.14.c.5.2.	
5th Field Co. R.E.	H.8.c.6.7.	
226th Field Co. R.E.	V.25.c.7.8.	
483rd Field Co. R.E.	C.20.b.9.9.	
5th Inf. Bde.	C.6.b.9.2.	
24th R. Fusiliers.	V.25.d.3.3.	
2nd Oxf. & Bucks L.I.	D.1.c.5.1.	
2nd H.L.I.	C.6.b.9.4.	
5th L.T.M. Battery.	C.6.d.9.9.	
6th Inf. Bde.	A.30.c.0.0.	
17th R. Fusiliers.	A.30.c.5.4.	
1st King's Regt.	G.3.a.6.4.	
2nd S. Staffs. Regt.	G.6.a.50.99.	
6th L.T.M. Battery.	G.5.a.4.9.	
99th Inf. Bde.	C.13.d.1.5.	
23rd R. Fusiliers.	C.21.a.5.1.	
1st R. Berks.	C.13.d.1.5.	
1st K.R.R.C.	C.13.c.55.25.	
99th L.T.M. Battery.	C.13.c.9.0.	
No.2 M.G. Battalion.	C.20.b.9.5.	
10th D.C.L.I. (Pioneers)	V.25.d.20.45.	
A.D.M.S.	SERANVILLERS	H.14.d.3.1.
5th Field Ambulance	C.12.b.3.7.	
6th Field Ambulance	FORENVILLE	H.8.c.6.9.
100th Field Ambulance	LA TARGETTE	(Div. Rest Station).
Bearers		C.13.d.0.0.
D.A.D.O.S.	LA TARGETTE	
D.A.P.M.	SERANVILLERS	H.19.b.9.8.
VI Corps H.Q.	GRAND CHANTEMEL	E.5 Central.
Guards Division.	BOUSSIERES	C.20.b.8.6.
62nd Division.	BEVILLERS	C.22.c.5.2.
S.A.A. Section.	BOUSSIERES	C.21.c. P.T.O.

APPENDIX LVII

- 2 -

3rd Division.	
8th Inf. Bde.	H.12.c.8.9.
9th Inf. Bde.	H.12.a.8.4.
76th Inf. Bde.	C.28.b.7.8.
	D.18.a.5.8.
19th Division.	
56th Inf. Bde.	ST AUBERT.
57th Inf. Bde.	-do-
58th Inf. Bde.	V.11.b.1.4.
	-do-
12th Tank Battalion.	QUIEVY.

R.W.Harrison
Captain,
for Lieut. Colonel,
General Staff, 2nd Division.

"A" Form.
MESSAGES AND SIGNALS.

Army Form C. 2121.
(In pads of 100.)

APPENDIX LVIII

TO: 5" Inf. Bde.
2" M.G. Batty
C.R.A

Sender's Number.	Day of Month.	In reply to Number.	
G.155	22	—	AAA

Secret aaa Zero on Oct 23rd will be at 03.20 aaa acknowledge.

From: 2nd Divn
Place:
Time: 12.25

(Signed) H.S. Knox Gore Major

APPENDIX LIX

Addendum No. 1 to 2nd Division Order No. 365.

22nd October, 1918.

1. With reference to para. 7 (a) (1), the opening line of the barrage for troops attacking VERTAIN will be W.20.central - W.14.b.5.0. and not as therein stated.

    The barrage will dwell on the opening line for 6 minutes.

    The troops attacking VERTAIN will form up 300 yds. West of this barrage.

2. The 5th Inf. Brigade will relieve the 1st and 3rd Guards Brigades in the line on the night October 22nd/23rd, relief probably being complete about 2200 hrs.

    Command of the Divisional Front will pass to G.O.C. 2nd Division on completion of relief.

    Command of the Artillery will pass to C.R.A. 2nd Division at 2100 hrs. October 22nd.

3. The 2nd Machine Gun Battalion will relieve the forward Machine Guns of the Guards Machine Gun Regiment on night 22nd/23rd October.

    The rear guns now in the SELLE Valley will be withdrawn at 2100 hrs.

4. The Reserve Battalion of the Left (3rd) Brigade Guards Division will be withdrawn at 2000 hrs. October 22nd.

5. On the RED LINE being reached a liaison post will be established between 5th and 57th Inf. Brigades about W.33.b.central.

6. P.O.W. Collecting Station will be near 5th Inf. Brigade Headquarters at ST. PYTHON, about V.29.d.7.5.

P.T.O.

- (2) -

7. ACKNOWLEDGE.

                                          E R Clayton
                                              Lieut-Colonel,
Issued to :-   General Staff, 2nd Division.

5th Inf. Brigade
6th Inf. Brigade
99th Inf. Brigade
No. 2 M.G. Battalion
C.R.A.
C.R.E.
2nd Signal Co. R.E.
10th D.C.L.I.
3rd Division
19th Division
62nd Division
VI Corps
84th H.A. Bde.
"Q" 2nd Division
A.D.M.S.
Guards Division.

LOCATIONS 2nd DIVISION   23 - 10 - 1918.

Reference Sheets :- 57b and 51 a, 1/40,000.

2nd Division H.Q.	O.12.b.6.7.
2nd Signal Coy.	O.12.b.65.70.
C.R.A.	O.12.b.4.7.
36th Bde. R.F.A.	Line.
41st Bde. R.F.A.	Line.
C.R.E.	O.12.b.0.4.
5th Field Coy.	ST VAAST.
226th Field Coy.	-do-
483rd Field Coy.	BOUSSIERES.
5th Infantry Brigade.	V.29.d.9.9.
2nd Oxf. & Bucks L.I.	V.30.a.6.2.
2nd H.L.I.	V.24.a.6.4.
24th R. Fusiliers.	W.19.c.1.8.
5th T.M. Battery.	ST PYTHON.
6th Infantry Brigade.	D.1.c.5.1.
1st Kings Regt.	O.12.a.75.60.
2nd S. Staffs Regt.	O.6.d.4.4.
17th R. Fusiliers.	O.6.d.2.6.
6th T.M. Battery.	O.6.d.5.2.
99th Infantry Brigade.	O.6.b.9.2.
1st R. Berks Regt.	O.6.b.9.2.
1st K.R.R.C.	O.12.b.6.8.
23rd R. Fusiliers.	ST PYTHON.
99th T.M. Battery.	O.6.d.9.9.
M.G. Battalion.	O.12.b.3.6.
10th D.C.L.I. (Pioneers)	ST VAAST.
A.D.M.S.	O.12.b.35.70.
Main Dressing Station.	V.25.d.2.3.
Adv. Dressing Station.	ST PYTHON.) V.30.c.7.4
2nd Div. Train H.Q.	SERANVILLERS.
S.A.A. Section H.Q.	O.15.c.5.0.
84th Bde. R.G.A.	D.13.a.88.50.

APPENDIX LX

- 2 -

```
D.A.P.M.            C.12.b.5.7.
                    (QUIEVY.         D.19.a.3.7.
3rd Division.       (Adv. ST PYTHON. V.29.d.8.8.
 8th Infantry Bde. E.1.a.8.6.

19th Division.      ST AUBERT.
 57th Inf. Bde.     V.5.c.9.1.
```

B.N. Harrison

Captain for,
Lieut. Colonel.
General Staff. 2nd Division.

"A" Form.
MESSAGES AND SIGNALS.

Army Form C. 2121.
(In pads of 100.)

WAR DIARY **APPENDIX LXI**

TO	O.C. Cyclists)
	O.C. Troop Oxford Hussars) By Hand
	5th Inf. Bde.

Sender's Number.	Day of Month.	In reply to Number.
G.9	23	AAA

Troop of Oxford Hussars and detachment of Cyclists now attached to 2nd Division will move at once to ST. PYTHON aaa O.C. Troop and O.C. Cyclists will report to O.C. Oxford Hussars at Headquarters 3rd Division D.5.b.6.5.

From: 2nd Division

Time: 1025

(sgd.) E.P.CLAYTON
G.S. Lt.Col

APPENDIX LXII

2ND DIVISION ORDER NO.344

SECRET

1. Should the attack develop favourably the Oxford Hussars, with a detachment of Corps Cyclists will be following up the enemy.

2. The following is the mission which is being given to the Oxford Hussars by the G.O.C. 3rd Division :-

   (i) To ascertain whether the crossings over the River Ecaillon in V1 Corps area are held by the enemy, and if possible to occupy them.

   (ii) To ascertain whether the following villages are held by the enemy :-

         BEAUDIGNIES (1V Corps area)
         RUESNES
         SEMERAIN (XV11 Corps area)

   (iii) To occupy RUESNES and the high ground in its vicinity to-night, pushing forward to the LE QUESNOY – VALENCIENNES Railway.

3. It is understood that at 1100 the troops of the 19th Division had reached Q.27.central and were about to push forward into ST. MARTIN under a barrage.

4. After the capture of the BROWN Line the 5th Infantry Brigade will push forward patrols towards the River ECAILLON and will, if possible, occupy the river crossings. Should BERMERAIN be unoccupied posts will be established to the North of the river. Should the Oxford Hussars occupy the village of RUESNES the 5th Infantry Brigade will push forward not less than one battalion to occupy the high ground in Q.24 with a second battalion in support North of the ECAILLON.

5. C.R.A. will arrange for artillery support to troops of the 2nd Division pushed forward North of the river.

6. O.C. Machine Gun Battalion will move forward one Company to support the troops North of the ECAILLON.

7. ACKNOWLEDGE.

23/10/18

                                  Lieut-Colonel
                          General Staff – 2nd Division

2ND DIVISION ORDER NO.366

Issued at 1200 to :-

Copy No.1 to 5th Inf. Bde.
" No.2 to 6th Inf. Bde.
" No.3   99th Inf. Bde.
" No.4   No.2 M.G. Battn.
" No.5   C.R.A.
" No.6   2nd Signal Coy.
" No.7   3rd Division
" No.8   19th Division
" No.9   VI Corps
" No.10   94th H.A. Bde.
" No.11   A.D.M.S.

"A" Form.
MESSAGES AND SIGNALS.

APPENDIX LXIII

TO: 2nd Division.

Sender's Number.	Day of Month.	In reply to Number.	AAA
G 242	23		

2nd Division will move support Brigade to neighbourhood of VERTAIN at once and Reserve Brigade to neighbourhood area ST PYTHON this evening AAA Acknowledge

From: 6th Corps
Time: 1220

"A" Form.
MESSAGES AND SIGNALS.

Army Form C. 2121.
(In pads of 100.)

APPENDIX LXIV

TO: 2nd Division.

Sender's Number.	Day of Month.	In reply to Number.	
G.241.	23		AAA

Warning order aaa VI Corps has been ordered to be prepared to capture tomorrow 24th Oct. as a main line of resistance the high ground running R.15.d.0.0 - R.14 central - R.3 central and to exploit forward from this line with Corps mounted troops supported by Infantry advanced guards aaa Flank Corps are co-operating aaa 3rd and 2nd Divisions will carry out the advance on the 6th Corps front AAA Dividing line between Divisions to be continued through road junction R.14.c.4.4 Road junction R.14.b.1.1 thence road to R.9.c.1.6 inclusive to 3rd Division AAA Corps mounted troops to be directed on VILLERS POL AAA 62nd and Guards Divisions will be prepared to close up their rear Brigades to QUIEVY and ST HILAIRE and ST VAAST respectively AAA Acknowledge AAA Addssd Divisions Corps Cavalry Regt Flank Corps Corps H.A. 12th Sq R.A.F. repeated remainder List B

From: 6th Corps
Place:
Time: 1225

"A" Form.
MESSAGES AND SIGNALS.

Army Form C. 2121.

PRIORITY

APPENDIX LXV

TO:
- 5th Bde
- 6th Bde
- 99th Bde
- C.R.A.
- C.R.E.
- "Q"
- A.D.M.S.
- D.A.P.M.
- Train
- M.Gun BN

Day of Month: 23   AAA

Following moves take place October 23rd aaa Details of M.G. Battn. at ST. HILAIRE will move at 1300 to ST. PYTHON aaa 6th Inf. Bde. will move to ST. PYTHON leaving ST. HILAIRE at 1500 aaa Bde. H.Q. to be established at V.29.d.8.8. lately occupied by 5th Inf. Bde. aaa Billets from Town Major.

From: 2nd Divn.
Time: 1355

(Z) G.S.

"A" Form.
MESSAGES AND SIGNALS.

Army Form C. 2121.
(In pads of 100.)

APPENDIX LXVI

Office of Origin and Service Instructions:
Operations
Priority to
5th & 99th Bde

TO: 5th Bde 6th Bde 99th Bde M.G.Battn. C.R.A. "Q" A.D.M.S. D.A.P.M. Signals. CRE

Sender's Number.	Day of Month.	In reply to Number.	
G.18	23		AAA

99th Brigade will move to VERTAIN area at once aaa Headquarters with 5th Bde at W.15.a.2.2. aaa 5th and 99th Bdes to ACKNOWLEDGE.

From Place: 2nd Divn.
Time: 1425

"A" Form.
MESSAGES AND SIGNALS.

Army Form C. 2121.
(In pads of 100.)

APPENDIX LXIX

TO	5" Bde	M.G. Batt	Signals
	6" "	CRA	Q
	99" "	CRE	ADMS

Sender's Number.	Day of Month.	In reply to Number.	AAA
G.30	23		

Zero October 24th will be 04.00 hours aaa acknowledge.

From: 2nd Div
Time: 19.20

E R Clayton Lt Col

"A" Form.
MESSAGES AND SIGNALS.

Army Form C. 2121.
(In pads of 100.)

APPENDIX Lxx

URGENT PRIORITY
99th Bde 3rd Divn
M.G. Bn

TO:
| 99th Bde | 3rd Divn | M.Gun Bn |
| C.R.A. | 61st Divn | 84th Bde R.G.A. |

Sender's Number: G 34
Day of Month: 23
In reply to Number: AAA

Reference G 29 barrage for attack of 99th Bde will be as follows aaa Opening line on ECAILLON River dwelling for 24 minutes aaa Creeps forward 100 yds in 6 minutes to a line 400 yds beyond the high bank of the river aaa Halts there one hour aaa Then moves forward 100 yds in 4 minutes to the line of the hedge passing through Q.18 and R.13 aaa Forward of this barrage advances at the rate of 100 yds in 6 minutes. aaa ACKNOWLEDGE

From: 2nd Divn
Time: 2025

(sd) E. R. CLAYTON Lt. Col
G.S.

"A" Form.
MESSAGES AND SIGNALS.

Army Form C. 2121.

APPENDIX LXXI

TO	5th Bde.	M.G. Battn.	4th Bde.	R.G.A.
	6th Bde.	C.R.A.	3rd Divn.	6th Corps
	99th Bde.	C.R.E.	61st Divn.	Signals

| Sender's Number. | Day of Month. | In reply to Number. | |
| G 35 | 23 | | AAA |

In continuation of G 29 outposts will be pushed out on to high ground across the railway by 99th Bde AAA Corps mounted troops are being directed on VILLERS POL under orders of G.O.C. 3rd Division AAA 99th Bde will consolidate position when reached AAA Plane will call for flares at 0700 and 0900 AAA 99th Bde M.Gun Bn to acknowledge.

From 2nd Divn
Time 2030

(sd) E.R. CLAYTON Lt Col.

G.S.

APPENDIX LXXII

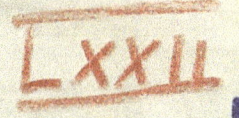

LOCATIONS 2ND DIVISION

Ref. Sheets 51.a & 57.b 1/40,000.   Moving at 0630 to

2nd Division H.Q.	ST HILAIRE	C.12.b.6.7.	(ST PYTHON
2nd Signal Coy.	C.12.b.65.70.		(D.6.a.95.40.
C.R.A.	C.12.b.4.7.		-do-
36th Bde. R.F.A.	Line.		-do-
41st Bde. R.F.A.	Line.		
C.R.E.	C.12.b.0.4.		-do-
5th Field Coy.	ST VAAST		
226th Field Coy.	ST VAAST		
483rd Field Coy.	D.1.c.6.5.		VERTAIN
5th Inf. Brigade.	W.15.a.2.2.		
2nd Oxf. & Bucks L.I.)			
2nd H.L.I.)			
24th R. Fusiliers.)	VERTAIN AREA.		
5th T.M. Battery.)			
6th Inf. Brigade.	D.6.a.4.3.		
1st Kings Regt.)			
2nd S. Staffs Regt.)	ST PYTHON AREA.		
17th R. Fusiliers.)			
6th T.M. Battery.)			
99th Inf. Brigade.	W.15.a.2.2.		
1st R. Berks Regt.)			
1st K.R.R.C.)	Line.		
23rd R. Fusiliers.)			
99th T.M. Battery.)			
M.G. Battalion.	D.5.b.9.5.		
10th D.C.L.I. (Pioneers)	D.6.a.1.9.		
A.D.M.S.	C.12.b.35.70.		ST PYTHON.
Main Dressing Station.	ST VAAST	V.25.d.2.3.	
Adv. Dressing Station.	VERTAIN.	W.15.c.6.5.	
5th Field Amb.	VERTAIN.		
6th Field Amb.	ST PYTHON.		
100th Field Amb.	ST VAAST.		
2nd Div. Train H.Q.	ST HILAIRE.		
D.A.P.M.	ST PYTHON.		
S.A.A. Section.	V.25.c.1.1.		
D.A.D.S.S.	ST HILAIRE.		
Bulk Canteen.	D.1.c.6.4.	ST HILAIRE	
P. of W. Collecting Stat.	W.15.a.2.2.		
P. of W. Cage.	V.30.c.7.3.		
84th Bde R.G.A.	C.15.c.3.2.		
VI Corps H.Q.	GRAND CHANTEMEL.		
3rd Division.	E.1.c.6.9.		
61st Division.	ST AUBERT.		

24/10/18

B. H. Lawson
Captain for,
Lieut. Colonel.
General Staff, 2nd. Divn.

"A" Form.
MESSAGES AND SIGNALS.

Army Form C. 2121.
(In pads of 100.)

APPENDIX LXXIII

TO	5th Bde	MGBn	Q
	6th "	CRA	ADMS
	99th "	CRE	Signals

Sender's Number	Day of Month	In reply to Number	
G.46	24		AAA

6th Bde will move at once to VERTAIN taking over Headquarters of 99th Bde aaa 6th Bde to acknowledge aaa addsd Bde MGBn CRA CRE Q ADMS Signals

From 2nd Div
Time 08:00

SAGES AND SIGNALS.

~~APPENDIX~~

TO: 2nd DIVISION

Sender's Number: G.275
Day of Month: 24
In reply to Number:
AAA

RUESNES has been captured and 3rd Division is consolidating the high ground from R.21.b.8.1. to R.14.central as a main line of resistance in touch with N.Z. Division on the right AAA The 2nd Division is approaching the high ground from R.14.central to R.7.c. in touch with 61st Divn. on its left AAA 3rd and 2nd Divns. will take steps to drive the enemy East of the LE QUESNOY VALENCIENNES railway from R.16.central to R.1.d.5.0. AAA 2nd Divn. will clear MORTRY FARM R.8.c. AAA Beyond the railway G.O.C. 3rd Division will keep touch with the enemy with the Corps mounted troops supported by Infantry advanced guards AAA General direction of advance VILLERS POL - WARGNIES LE GRAND AAA Consolidation of main line of resistance will be proceeded with

"A" Form.
MESSAGES AND SIGNALS.

Army Form C. 2121.
(In pads of 100.)
No. of Message..........

Prefix........ Code........ m.	Words.	Charge.		Recd. at...... m.
Office of Origin and Service Instructions.			This message is on m/s of:	
	Sent			Date............
.......*........	At........m.		....................Service.	From............
....	To........			
	By........		(Signature of "Franking Officer.")	By............

TO

- 2 -

Sender's Number.	Day of Month.	In reply to Number.	
*			A A A

and main bodies will not be
advanced beyond this line without
further orders from Corps H.Q.
AAA ACKNOWLEDGE

From	Sixth Corps		
Place			
Time	1110.		

The above may be forwarded as now corrected. (Z)

.... Censor. Signature of Addressor or person authorised to telegraph in his name.

* This line, except **A A A**, should be erased if not required.

"A" Form.
MESSAGES AND SIGNALS.

Army Form C. 2121.
(In pads of 100.)

APPENDIX LXXV

TO: 2nd Division

Sender's Number: HL 212
Day of Month: 24

WARNING ORDER AAA As soon as 2nd and 3rd Divisions are established on line of resistance ordered in 6th Corps G. 280 of 23rd October Guards and 62nd Divisional Artilleries will revert to their own Divisions for rest and refit. AAA Lines to be selected as follows AAA Guards D.A. West of River SELLE AAA 62nd D.A. East of River SELLE near ST PYTHON AAA Town Major will allot any accommodation available AAA Guards and 62nd D.AC s will remain under 2nd and 3rd xxxx Divisional control till a time to be notifed later AAA

From: 6th Corps.
Time: 11.55.

Army Form C. 2121.
(In pads of 100.)

MESSAGES AND SIGNALS. No. of Message..........

APPENDIX LXXVI

| TO | 99th Brigade C.R.A. | | |

Sender's Number.	Day of Month.	In reply to Number.	
G. 51	24		A A A

61st Division report line at 1030 to run right Bde. LA FOLIE - MILL Q.16.d. - Western outskirts of ST. MARTIN AAA Left Bde. holding railway South of VENDEGIES with some troops in SOMMAING AAA Parties reported in Q.17.a. and b. AAA 99th Bde. will consolidate main line of resistance when gained and will hold line of the railway including MORTRY FARM with outposts

From: 2nd Division
Place:
Time: 1220.

(Z)

Sgd. E.R. CLAYTON, Lt. Col
GS.

"A" Form.
MESSAGES AND SIGNALS.

Army Form C. 2121.

APPENDIX LXXVII

TO 5th Bde 6th Bde 99th Bde. CRA CRE M.G. Battn. "Q" ADMS Signals DAPM Div. Train

Sender's Number.	Day of Month.	In reply to Number.	AAA
G. 53	24		

2 Battalions 5th Bde. will move to ST. PYTHON on afternoon of October 24th AAA 6th Bde. will move 2 Battalions to ESCARMAIN third Battalion will remain at VERTAIN AAA 5th and 6th Bdes. to ACKNOWLEDGE.

From 2nd Division
Place
Time 1300

Sgd. E.R. CLAYTON Lt Col
G3

"A" Form.
MESSAGES AND SIGNALS.

Army Form C. 2121.

URGENT
OPERATIONS
PRIORITY

APPENDIX LXXVII

TO	5th Bde	6th Bde	99th Bde
	C.R.A.	M.G.Bn	A.D.M.S.

Sender's Number	Day of Month	In reply to Number	
G 54	24		AAA

6th Bde will place one Battalion at disposal of 99th Bde at once to be used as reserve to 99th Bde or to cover left flank AAA

Addressed 6th and 99th Bdes repeated 5th Bde C.R.A. M.G.Bn A.D.M.S.

From Place: 2nd Divn

W J Knox Lt Major

"A" Form.
MESSAGES AND SIGNALS.

Army Form C. 2121.
(In pads of 100.)

APPENDIX LXXIX

Priority to
99th Bde. 6th Bde
M.G.Batt. C.R.A.

TO: 99th Bde | 6th Bde | A.D.M.S.
6th Bde | C.R.A.
M.G.Batt | Signals

Sender's Number: G.59.
Day of Month: 24

AAA

The line gained to-day is to be consolidated aaa enemy is to be harassed with Artillery and other arms, and touch maintained with him with patrols aaa Should the enemy show signs of withdrawing he is to be followed up until the line of the railway is reached where an outpost line should be established aaa The position held at present will be organised in depth and entrenched aaa The Battn of 6thBde at present under G.O.C. 99th Bde will revert to Command of G.O.C. 6th Bde. aaa Addressed 6th Bde. 99th Bde. C.R.A. M.G. Battn. repeated remainder List "A".

From: 2nd Div.
Time: 1800

APPENDIX LXXX

SECRET.

LOCATIONS 2ND DIVISION   25th October 1918.

Reference Sheet 57.b and 51.a.   1/40,000.

2nd Division H.Q.	ST PYTHON D.6.a.7.2.
2nd Signal Coy.	ST PYTHON
C.R.A.	ST PYTHON D.6.a.8.0.
36th Bde. R.F.A.)	
41st Bde R.F.A.)	Line.
C.R.E.	D.6.a.5.7.
5th Field Coy R.E.	ST VAAST. Moving to ESCARMAIN.
226th Field Coy R.E.	W.15.b.8.8.
483rd Field Coy R.E.	W.2.b.7.9.
5th Infantry Bde.	VERTAIN. W.15.a.7.2.
2nd Oxf. and Bucks L.I.	ST PYTHON.
2nd H.L.I.	VERTAIN.
24th R. Fusiliers.	ST PYTHON.
5th T.M. Battery.	ST PYTHON.
6th Inf. Brigade.	VERTAIN. W.15.a.7.2.
1st Kings Regt.	ESCARMAIN.
2nd S. Staffs. Regt.	-do-
17th R. Fusiliers.	VERTAIN.
6th T.M. Battery.	-do-
99th Infantry Bde.	ESCARMAIN. W.4.a.8.8.
1st R. Berks Regt.)	
1st K.R.R.C.)	
23rd R. Fusiliers.)	Line.
99th T.M. Battery.)	
M.G.Battalion.	D.5.b.9.5.
10th D.C.L.I. (Pioneers)	D.6.a.1.9.
A.D.M.S.	D.6.a.6.4.
Main Dressing Station.	VERTAIN. W.15.c.7.6.
Adv. Dressing Station.	CAPELLE. Q.35.a.9.8.
5th Field Ambulance.	W.15.c.7.6.
6th Field Ambulance.	VERTAIN.
100th Field Ambulance.	ST PYTHON.
D.A.D.O.S.	ST HILAIRE.
D.A.P.M.	ST PYTHON.
2nd Div. Train. H.Q.	ST HILAIRE.
S.A.A. Section H.Q.	V.30.b.6.0.

P.T.O.

84th Bde R.G.A.	D.5.b.90.25.
VI Corps H.Q.	GRAND CHANTEMEL.
Corps P. of W. Cage.	SOLESMES. (Hotel de Ville).
Guards Division.	BOUSSAERES.
62nd Division.	BEVILLERS.
3rd Division.	SOLESMES. E.1.c.5.9.
8th Inf. Bde.	W.5.b.1.0.
9th Inf. Bde.	W.17.d.1.8.
76th Inf. Bde.	W.21.d.5.9.
61st Division.	MONTRECOURT.

R. N. Hanson
Captain for
Lieut Colonel.
General Staff. 2nd Division.

"A" Form.
MESSAGES AND SIGNALS.

Army Form C. 2121.
(In pads of 100.)

WAR DIARY.

APPENDIX LXXXI

TO: **2nd Division.**

Sender's Number.	Day of Month.	In reply to Number.	
H/213	25		AAA

Refce 6 Corps wire H.212 of 24th October aaa Guards and 62nd DAS will revert forthwith to their own Divns for Rest and refit under mutual arrangements of Divns aaa DACS will revert to their own Divns when no longer required by Divns in line aaa Battery positions will be ckeared as follows by Guards DA to 2nd Div ARP at W.9.c.3.7. by 62nd DA under orders of 3rd DA aaa Addsd all recipients of H.212.

From
Place: **6 Corps.**
Time:

(Z)

"A" Form.
MESSAGES AND SIGNALS.

WAR DIARY.

APPENDIX LXXXII

TO: 2nd Division.

Sender's Number: G.308
Day of Month: 25
AAA

6th Corps has reached the following general line R.10.c.--LA CROISETTE(R.3.c.)- R.2.cent in touch with Divs on both flanks aaa A few Germans are still on the Rly about R.16.cent aaa Steps are being taken by 3rd and N.Z. Divs to round them up aaa 3rd Div will take over the duties of advanced Guard on the whole Corps front at daylight tomorrow 26th Oct passing through the troops of 2nd Div now in the line aaa Corps mounted troops 3rd Div Arty 76th Bde RFA and one Mobile Bde RGA will be under the orders of GOC 3rd Div aaa Advanced guard will follow up and maintain touch with the enemy but will not carry out an attack without reference to Corps HQ aaa Following will be Corps boundaries for the present aaa Right Boundary R.22.a.0.0.--R.11.cent-M.1.b.cent-G.32.cent-R.25.cent.- aaa Left Boundaries R.7.a.7.2.--L.32.d.0.0.--L.28.a.0.0.--L.17.b.2.3.-L.12.c.0.0.--G.2.cent-A.17.a.3.0.--A.12 cent aaa After 3rd Div has passed through 2nd Div will be responsible for the organisation maintainence and defence of the Corps main line of resistance in the left Divl sector and when 3rd Div has passed beyond the line of resistance in the right sector will be

"A" Form.
MESSAGES AND SIGNALS.

Army Form C. 2121.
(In pads of 100.)

TO -6th Corps G.308 contd-

AAA

responsible for the line on the whole Corps
front aaa 2nd Divl Arty and 14th Army Bde RHA
will remain in observation to cover main line
of resistance under GOC 2nd Divn aaa ACKNOWLEDGE
aaa Addsd 2nd and 3rd Divns reptd remainder list
"B"

From: 6th Corps.
Place: 1910 hrs.

URGENT OPERATIONS PRIORITY to :-   SECRET.

6th Brigade	2nd Signal Co.
99th Brigade	3rd Division
M.G. Battalion	61st Division
C.R.A.	

D.R.L.S. to :-

5th Brigade	Vl Corps
C.R.E.	84th Bde. R.G.A.
10th D.C.L.I.	"Q" 2nd Division
	A.D.M.S.

G. 80   25/10

3rd Division is taking over duties of advanced guard on the whole Corps front at daylight October 26th AAA Corps Mounted Troops 3rd Div. Artillery and one Mobile Brigade R.G.A. will be under orders of G.O.C. 3rd Division AAA The orders to 3rd Division are to follow up and maintain touch with the enemy but not to attack if organised resistance is met without reference to Vl Corps AAA 99th Brigade will remain responsible for defence organisation and maintenance of Corps main line of resistance in present Divisional Sector AAA When whole of 3rd Division has passed through the line of resistance on whole Corps front will be taken over by 99th Brigade AAA 8th Inf. Brigade are relieving 99th Brigade in front of main line of resistance in present Divisional Sector on October 26th arrangements for relief to be made between Brigadiers AAA Relief to be completed by 1000 hrs. AAA 99th Brigade can withdraw one Battalion to CAPELLE two Battalions will remain in area North of ECAILLON River after relief on October 26th AAA After 3rd Division has passed through 2nd Div. Artillery and 14th Bde. R.H.A. will remain in observation to cover whole of main line of resistance AAA Following are the Corps boundaries AAA Right boundary R.22.a.0.0. R.11.central - M.1.b. cent. . . . G.32.central - G.11.central - B.25.central AAA Left Boundary R.7.a.7.2. - L.32.d.0.0. - L.28.a.0.0. - L.17.b.5.3. - L.12.c.0.0. - G.2.central - A.17.a.3.0. - A.12.central

                                        E.R. Clayton
                                        Lieut-Colonel,
                                        General Staff, 2nd Division.

Issued at :- 1940 hrs.

APPENDIX LXXXIV

SECRET.

LOCATIONS 2ND DIVISION.   26th October 1918.

Reference Sheet 57.b. and 51.a.   1/40,000.

2nd Division H.Q.	ST PYTHON. D.6.a.7.2.
2nd Signal Coy.	-do-
C.R.A.	ST PYTHON. D.6.a.8.0.
36th Bde. R.F.A.)	
41st Bde. R.F.A.)	Line
C.R.E.	D.6.a.5.7.
5th Field Coy. R.E.	W.4.d.6.6.
226th Field Coy. R.E.	W.15.b.8.8.
483rd Field Coy. R.E.	W.2.b.7.9.
5th Infantry Brigade.	VERTAIN. W.15.a.7.2.
2nd Oxf. and Bucks L.I.	ST PYTHON.
2nd H.L.I.	VERTAIN.
24th R. Fusiliers.	ST PYTHON.
5th T.M. Battery.	-do-
6th Infantry Brigade.	VERTAIN. W.15.a.7.2.
1st Kings Regt.	ESCARMAIN. W.4.d.9.9.
2nd S. Staffs. Regt.	-do- W.4.b.9.1.
17th R. Fusiliers.	VERTAIN. W.15.b.2.7.
6th T.M. Battery.	-do- W.15.a.4.1.
99th Infantry Brigade.	ESCARMAIN. W.4.d.8.8.
1st R. Berks Regt.)	
1st K.R.R.C.)	Line.
23rd R. Fusiliers.)	
99th T.M. Battery.)	
M.G. Battalion.	D.5.b.9.5.
10th D.C.L.I.(Pioneers)	W.15.a.8.4.
A.D.M.S.	D.6.a.6.4.
Main Dressing Station.	VERTAIN. W.15.c.7.6.
Adv. Dressing Station.	CAPELLE. Q.35.a.9.8.
5th Field Ambulance.	W.15.c.7.6.
6th Field Ambulance.	VERTAIN.
100th Field Ambulance.	ST PYTHON.
D.A.D.O.S.	ST PYTHON.
D.A.P.M.	ST PYTHON.

P.T.O.

```
2nd Div. Train H.Q.         ST PYTHON.
Div. Reception Camp.        Billet 11. BOUSSIERES.
Div. P. of W. Cage.         VERTAIN. W.15.a.2.3.

S.A.A. Section. H.Q.        V.30.b.6.0.

84th Bde. R.G.A.            D.5.b.90.25.

VI Corps H.Q.               GRAND CHANTEMEL.
Corps P. of W. Cage.        SOLESMES. (Hotel de Ville.)

Guards Division.            BOUSSIERES.

62nd Division.              BEVILLERS.

3rd Division.               SOLESMES. E.1.c.5.9.
  8th Inf. Brigade.         W.5.b.1.0.
  9th Inf. Brigade.         W.5.d.1.6.
  76th Inf. Brigade.        W.21.b.4.0.

61st Division.              VENDEGIES. Q.14.d.
  182nd Inf. Brigade.       P.30.c.2.1.
  183rd Inf. Brigade.)
  184th Inf. Brigade.)      MAISON BLEUE. Q.31.b.8.9.
```

B. H. Harrison

Captain for,
Lieut. Colonel.
General Staff. 2nd Division.

APPENDIX LXXXV

LOCATIONS 2nd Division 27th October, 1918.

Reference Sheet 57b and 51a 1/40,000

Unit	Location	Grid
2nd Division H.Q.	ST PYTHON	D.6.a.7.2.
5th Inf. Brigade.	VERTAIN	W.15.a.7.8.
2nd Oxf. and Bucks L.I.	ST PYTHON	D.6.a.3.8.
2nd H.L.I.	VERTAIN	W.15.c.9.8.
24th Royal Fusiliers	ST PYTHON	D.6.a.6.5.
5th L.T.M. Battery	- " -	V.30.c.5.0.
6th Inf. Brigade	VERTAIN	W.15.a.7.2.
1st King's Regt.	ESCARMAIN	W.4.d.9.9.
2nd S. Staffs. Regt.	- " -	W.4.b.9.1.
17th Royal Fusiliers	VERTAIN	W.15.b.2.7.
6th L.T.M. Batty.	- " -	W.15.a.4.1.
99th Inf. Brigade.	CAPELLE	Q.35.a.7.5.
1st Royal Berks Regt.		Q.28.b.7.8.
1st K.R.R.C.		Q.13.d.8.4.
23rd Royal Fusiliers		Q.35.a.5.7.
99th L.T.M. Batty.		Q.35.a.6.8.

Otherwise no change since last report.

Unit	Location	Grid
3rd Division.	SOLESMES.	E.1.c.5.9.
8th Inf. Brigade.		W.5.b.1.0.
9th Inf. Brigade.		W.5.d.1.6.
76th Inf. Brigade.	ESCARMAIN.	
61st Division.	VENDEGIES.	Q.14.d.
182nd Inf. Brigade		P.30.c.2.1.
183rd Inf. Brigade.	MAISON BLEUE.	Q.31.b.8.9.
184th Inf. Brigade.		Q.16.a.4.2.

Captain for,
Lieut. Colonel.
General Staff. 2nd Divn.

'G' Diary

APPENDIX LXXXVI

Army Form W.3815.

STRENGTH RETURN MADE UP TO 12 NOON SATURDAY 26th October 1918.

3rd Corps (Division).

UNIT.	(i.) Strength for previous week, compiled in accordance with A.G.'s instructions.		(ii.) Increase during week, due to drafts, etc., taken on strength of Unit.		(iii.) Totals from (i.) and (ii.)		(iv.) Decrease during week—casualties, etc., deducted from strength of Unit.		"A" Strength, excluding Attached.		"B" Not present with the Unit and not at the disposal of C.O. Included in column "A."		"A minus B." Available Fighting Strength, including Personnel of Battalion Transport and Quartermaster's Stores.		REMARKS. (Brief notes regarding (iii), (iv), and "B", etc.)
	Officers.	O.R.	Officers.	O.R.	Officers.	O.R.	Officers.	O.R.	Officers.	O.R.	Officers.	O.R.	Officers.	O.R.	
8th INFANTRY BRIGADE.															
2nd Royal Fusiliers.	39	761	1	3	40	764	3	24	37	740	15	160	22	580	
5th Oxf. & Bucks L.I.	48	787	—	115	48	902	4	66	44	836	11	138	33	698	
2nd Highland L.I.	34	895	2	15	37	910	1	34	36	876	9	140	27	736	
Total Brigade.	121	2343	4	133	125	2576	8	124	117	2452	35	438	82	2014	
9th INFANTRY BRIGADE.															
1st Royal Fusiliers.	32	639	4	17	36	656	1	28	35	628	9	110	26	518	
1st King's Regiment.	32	756	5	22	36	778	1	11	35	767	12	118	23	649	
2nd S. Staffs Regt.	32	807	—	22	35	829	1	7	34	822	15	124	19	698	
Total Brigade.	96	2203	9	61	107	2263	3	46	104	2217	36	352	68	1865	
99th INFANTRY BRIGADE.															
22nd Royal Fusiliers.	35	734	3	7	38	741	1	45	37	696	11	132	26	564	
1st Royal Berks Regt.	35	702	—	34	35	736	4	98	31	638	10	101	21	537	
1st K.R. Rifle Corps.	36	653	6	105	42	758	1	29	41	729	14	119	27	610	
Total Brigade.	106	2089	9	146	115	2236	6	172	109	2063	35	352	74	1711	
Pioneer Battalion.															
10th D.C.L.I.	30	795	—	3	30	798	1	15	29	785	8	59	21	724	
TOTAL DIVISION.	356	7550	22	321	377	7840	18	319	359	7537	114	1181	245	6356	
No.2 M.G. Corps.	46	898	2	15	47	910	1	17	46	893	8	81	38	812	

(Sgd) E. Armstrong
for Major General,
Commanding 3rd Division.

[P.T.O.

CHANGES IN NOMINAL ROLLS OF OFFICERS.

(*i.e.*, Explanation of Increases and Decreases.)

Unit.	Joined.	Struck Off.	Cause.

NOMINAL ROLL of OFFICERS will be forwarded as soon as Names are available.

EXPLANATION OF INCREASE AND DECREASE.
OTHER RANKS.

UNIT:	INCREASE.	DECREASE.
5th INFANTRY BRIGADE.		
24th Royal Fusiliers.	8 From hospital.	17 Wounded.
		7 Evacuated sick.
2nd Oxf. & Bucks L.I.	115 Reinforcements.	8 Killed.
		44 Wounded.
		3 Missing.
		3 Wounded and Missing.
		6 Evacuated sick.
2nd Highland L.I.	18 Reinforcements.	27 Battle casualties.
		6 Evacuated sick.
		1 to Base Depot.
6th INFANTRY BRIGADE.		
17th Royal Fusiliers.	18 Reinforcements.	14 Evacuated sick.
	2 From hospital.	12 Wounded.
		1 Commission.
		1 Base Depot.
1st King's Regiment.	22 Reinforcements.	1 Base Depot.
		10 Evacuated sick.
2nd S.Staffs Regt.	22 Reinforcements.	1 Wounded.
		5 Evacuated sick.
		1 to 6th T.M.Battery.
99th INFANTRY BRIGADE.		
23rd Royal Fusiliers.	7 Reinforcements.	31 Est.casualties.
		12 Evacuated sick.
		2 Commissions.
1st Royal Berks Regt.	10 Reinforcements.	50 Est.casualties.
	4 From hospital.	1 Base Depot.
		1 Commission.
		6 Evacuated sick.
1st K.R.Rifle Corps.	103 Reinforcements.	22 Evacuated sick.
		2 Wounded.
		1 To England on compassionate grounds.
		1 Commission.
10th D.C.L.I.(Pioneers)	3 From hospital.	1 Wounded.
		12 Evacuated sick.
No.2 Bn. M.G.Corps.	12 Reinforcements.	10 Casualties.
	3 From hospital.	6 Evacuated sick.
		1 Died in U.K.while on leave.

EXPLANATION OF COLUMN "B".

(a) On leave.
(b) Sick.
(c) Attending Courses.
(d) Detailed for specific duties etc.
(e) Extra regimentally employed.

UNIT.

5th INFANTRY BRIGADE.

24th Royal Fusiliers.		Off.	O.R.	
	(a)	7	101	
	(b)	2	6	
	(c)	-	6	
	(d)	* -	-	*2 Officers not yet joined.
	(e)	6	48	
		15	160	

2nd Oxf. & Bucks L.I.	(a)	5	74
	(b)	-	9
	(c)	3	8
	(d)	1	-
	(e)	2	47
		11	138

2nd Highland L.I.	(a)	5	60
	(b)	2	8
	(c)	1	11
	(d)	-	-
	(e)	1	41
		9	120

6th INFANTRY BRIGADE.

17th Royal Fusiliers.	(a)	5	54
	(b)	2	5
	(c)	2	10
	(d)	-	2
	(e)	-	39
		9	110

1st King's Regiment.	(a)	6	71
	(b)	2	9
	(c)	2	11
	(d)	-	1
	(e)	2	26
		12	118

2nd S.Staffs Regt.				
	(a)	6	56	
	(b)	5	5	
	(c)	2	22	
	(d)	-	3	
	(e)	* 2	38	XXXXXXXX
		15	124	

99th INFANTRY BRIGADE.

23rd Royal Fusiliers.	(a)	3	68
	(b)	2	10
	(c)	2	11
	(d)	-	2
	(e)	4	41
		11	132

1st Royal Berks Regt.				
	(a)	1	46	
	(b)	4	5	
	(c)	3	15	
	(d)	-	-	
	(e)	* 2	35	* Not yet joined.
		10	101	

P.T.O.

99th INFANTRY BRIGADE (Cont'd)   Off. O.R.
1st K.R.Rifle Corps.   (a)   6   40
                          (b)   2   18
                          (c)   2   22
                          (d)   -   3
                          (e)   * 4   36   * 1 Officer sent to Base for
                                 --   ---   disposal.
                                 14   119
                                 ==   ===

10th D.C.L.I.(Pioneers)   (a)   6   31
                          (b)   1   9
                          (c)   -   10
                          (d)   -   -
                          (e)   1   9
                                 --   --
                                  8   59
                                 ==   ==

No.2 Bn. M.G.Corps.   (a)   8   59
                          (b)   -   17
                          (c)   -   4
                          (d)   -   -
                          (e)   -   1
                                 --   --
                                  8   81
                                 ==   ==

"A" Form.
MESSAGES AND SIGNALS.

Army Form C. 2121.
(In pads of 100.)

URGENT
OPERATIONS

APPENDIX
LXXXVII

TO: 2nd Division.

Sender's Number: G 349
Day of Month: 27
AAA

3rd Division will take over responsibility for the main line of resistance in the left sector to-night from the 2nd Division AAA Artillery in observation covering above line will come under orders of G.O.C. 3rd Division on completion of relief AAA Details of relief to be arranged between Divisions concerned AAA On relief 2nd Division will be support Division in the area ROMERIES VERTAIN ST PYTHON SOLESMES AAA Area East of ESCARMAIN inclusive is allotted to 3rd Divn AAA Divnl H.Q. will remain as at ~~present~~ AAA ACKNOWLEDGE.

From: 6th Corps
Time: 1254

"A" Form.
MESSAGES AND SIGNALS.

Army Form C. 2121.

APPENDIX LXXXVIII

TO:
5" Bde	Q	3" Div
6" "	A.D.M.S	
99 "	D.A.P.M	

Sender's Number: G.105
Day of Month: 27

6" Bde will move two Battns from ESCARMAIN to ROMERIES on October 27" not to enter ROMERIES before 16.00 aaa added 6" Bde. repto 5" + 99" Bdes. Q. ADMS. DAPM. + 3" Div

From: 2" Div
Time: 3.50

Sig. D.R. Clayton

"A" Form.
MESSAGES AND SIGNALS.

Army Form C. 2121.
(In pads of 100.)

APPENDIX LXXXIX

TO	5th Bde	M.Gun Bn	Signals	A.D.M.S.
	6th Bde	C.R.A.	Train	3rd Divn
	99th Bde	C.R.E.	"Q"	

Sender's Number.	Day of Month.	In reply to Number.	
G 106	27		AAA

3rd Divn is taking over the whole of the Corps front with forward area AAA 99th Bde will be relieved by 76th Bde to-night AAA Details of relief to be arranged between Brigadiers AAA On completion 99th Bde will move to ~~SOLONNES~~ SOLESMES AAA 99th Bde to acknowledge AAA Addressed 99th Bde repeated 6th Bde 5th Bde M.Gun Bn C.R.A. C.R.E. Signals Train "Q" A.D.M.S. 3rd Divn.

From: 2nd Divn
Time: 1430

(Z) (sd) R.C.FIREBRACE. Major

"A" Form.
MESSAGES AND SIGNALS.

Army Form C. 2121.
(In pads of 100.)

APPENDIX XC

TO:
- 5th Bde. — O.R.A. — Train.
- 6th Bde. — O.R.E. — Signals.
- 99th Bde. — "Q" — 3rd Div.

Sender's Number: G.108.   Day of Month: 27   AAA

The Command of the Artillery covering the Corps sector will pass to G.O.C. 3rd D.A. at 1000 28th Oct. aaa Addressed all recipients of G.108.

From: 2nd Div.
Time: 1550.

APPENDIX XCI

2nd Division No. G.U. 4/11.

5th Inf. Brigade	Signal Co.
6th Inf. Brigade	2nd Div. Train
99th Inf. Brigade	10th D.C.L.I.
M.G. Battalion	"Q"
C.R.A.	A.D.M.S.
C.R.E.	D.A.P.M.

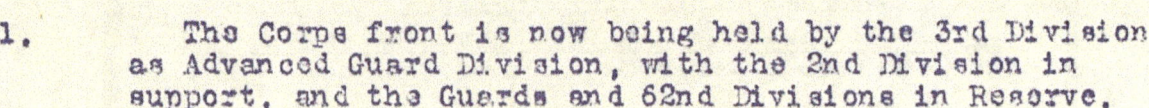

SECRET

1. The Corps front is now being held by the 3rd Division as Advanced Guard Division, with the 2nd Division in support, and the Guards and 62nd Divisions in Reserve.

2. It is probable that on the night of October 29th/30th 2nd Division will relieve 3rd Division as Advanced Guard Division. If this relief is carried out the 6th Brigade will relieve the 8th Inf. Brigade in the Right Section of the Corps front, and the 5th Inf. Brigade the 76th Inf. Brigade in the Left Section.

3. The 99th Brigade will be in Reserve at ESCARMAIN.

4. Brigadiers will arrange for necessary reconnaissances to be carried out.

5. The Area allotted to the Division when this relief has taken place will be East of ESCARMAIN inclusive, with Divisional Headquarters at ST. PYTHON.

E R Clayton
Lieut-Colonel,
General Staff, 2nd Division.

27th October, 1918.

"A" Form.
MESSAGES AND SIGNALS.

Army Form C. 2121.
(In pads of 100.)

APPENDIX XCII

TO: 2nd Divn

Sender's Number: G 365
Day of Month: 28
AAA

Reliefs & moves ordered in 6th Corps N.o 398 are postponed 24 hours aaa Acknowledge aaa Added recipients N o 398

From: 6th Corps
Time: 10.15

APPENDIX XCIII

SECRET.

LOCATIONS 2ND DIVISION.   29th October 1918.

Reference Sheet 57b and 51a.   1/40,000.

2nd Division H.Q.	ST PYTHON. D.6.a.7.2.
2nd Signal Coy.	ST PYTHON.
C.R.A.	ST PYTHON. D.6.a.8.0.
36th Bde. R.F.A.)	
41st Bde. R.F.A.)	Line.
C.R.E.	D.6.a.5.7.
5th Field Coy. R.E.	Q.29.c.3.1.
226th Field Coy. R.E.	W.15.b.8.8.
483rd Field Coy. R.E.	W.2.b.7.9.
5th Infantry Brigade.	VERTAIN. W.15.a.7.2.
2nd Oxf. & Bucks L.I.	ST PYTHON.
2nd H.L.I.	VERTAIN.
24th R. Fusiliers.	ST PYTHON.
5th T.M. Battery.	ST PYTHON.
6th Infantry Brigade.	VERTAIN. W.15.a.7.2.
1st Kings Regt.	ROMERIES. W.21.d.80.83.
2nd S.Staffs. Regt.	ROMERIES. W.21.d.7.9.
17th R. Fusiliers.	VERTAIN.
6th T.M. Battery.	VERTAIN.
99th Infantry Brigade.	SOLESMES. E.1.c.5.2.
1st R. Berks. Regt.)	
1st K.R.R.C.)	SOLESMES.
23rd R. Fusiliers.)	
99th T.M. Battery.)	
M.G. Battalion.	D.5.b.9.5.
"A" Company.	ST PYTHON. D.6.a.3.6.
"B" "	VERTAIN. W.15.a.9.3.
"C" "	STPYTHON. V.30.c.6.1.
"D" "	ST PYTHON. D.6.a.3.7.
10th D.C.L.I.(Pioneers)	W.15.a.8.4.
2nd Div. Reception Camp.	BOUSSIERES. Haupt St. Billet No.14a.
Railhead Reception Camp.	CAMBRAI ANNEXE Station.
D.A.D.O.S.	ST PYTHON.
D.A.P.M.	ST PYTHON.
2nd Div. Train H.Q.	ST PYTHON.
S.A.A. Section H.Q.	V.30.b.6.0.

P.T.O.

A.D.M.S.	D.6.a.6.4.
Main Dressing Station.	VERTAIN. W.15.c.7.6.
Adv. Dressing Station.	CAPELLE. Q.35.a.9.8.
5th Field Ambulance.	W.15.c.7.6.
6th Field Ambulance.	VERTAIN.
100th Field Ambulance.	ST PYTHON.
84th Bde. R.G.A.	D.5.b.90.25.
VI Corps H.Q.	GRAND CHANTEMEL.
Corps P. of W. Cage.	SOLESMES. (Hotel de Ville.)
Guards Division.	BOUSSIERES.
62nd Division.	BEVILLERS.
3rd Division.	SOLESMES. E.1.c.6.8.
8th Infantry Brigade.	RUESNES. R.20.b.1.6.
9th Infantry Brigade.	W.5.d.1.6.
76th Infantry Brigade.	CAPELLE. Q.35.a.6.7.
61st Division.	VENDEGIES. Q.14.d.1.7.
182nd Infantry Brigade.	VENDEGIES. Q.8.d.8.7.
183rd Infantry Brigade.	LARBLIN. Q.16.a.
184th Infantry Brigade.	BERMERAIN. Q.22.a.5.2.

R. H. Hamilton
Captain for
Lieut. Colonel,
General Staff. 2nd Divn.

"A" Form.
MESSAGES AND SIGNALS.

Army Form C. 2121.
(In pads of 100.)

APPENDIX XCIV

TO: 2nd Divn

Sender's Number.	Day of Month.	In reply to Number.	
G.380	28		AAA

6th Corps. G.365 is cancelled aaa Reliefs and moves outlined in 6th Corps No.398 will take place as forecasted aaa orders follow aaa added recipients G.365.

From: 6th Corps
Time: 22.30

"A" Form.
MESSAGES AND SIGNALS.

Army Form C. 2121.
(In pads of 100.)

APPENDIX XCV

TO	5" Bde	M.G. Bn	DAPM
	6 "	Q	3rd Div
	99 "	Signals	

Sender's Number: G.122
Day of Month: 28

Relief ordered in 2nd Div GU. 4/11 will take place on October 29/30th aaa 99" Bde will leave SOLESMES at 10.00 hours & will move to ESCARMAIN relieving 9" Bde which moves to SOLESMES aaa 99" Bde will come under orders of 3rd Div until relief is complete aaa 99" Bde to acknowledge

From: 2nd Div
Time: 23.25

(Signed) E.R. Clayton Lt Col

"A" Form.
MESSAGES AND SIGNALS.

APPENDIX XCVI

TO: 6" Bde

Sender's Number: G.123
Day of Month: 28

6" Bde will relieve 8" Bde in the line on Oct. 29/30" not to pass VERTAIN before 14.00 hours aaa Detailed orders follow—

From: 2nd Divn
Time: 23.30

Signed E.R. Clayton Lt Col

"A" Form.
MESSAGES AND SIGNALS.

Army Form C. 2121.
(In pads of 100.)

APPENDIX XCVII

TO: 5ᵗʰ Bde

Sender's Number: G.125
Day of Month: 29
In reply to Number: —
AAA

5ᵗʰ Bde will relieve 76ᵗʰ Bde today aaa 5ᵗʰ Bde not to pass VERTAIN before 15.30 aaa Acknowledge

From: 2ⁿᵈ Div
Place:
Time: 08.45

Signed E R Clayton
Lt Col
45

SECRET.

2nd DIVISION ORDER No. 367.   29th October, 1918.

APPENDIX XCVIII

1. The 2nd Division will relieve the 3rd Division as Advanced Guard Division on October 29th/30th.

2. The 3rd Division is at present in touch with the enemy holding the following line :-

    Outpost Line - R.16.d.2.7. (in touch with New Zealand Division.
    R.10.a. and c., R.3.a. and c., R.2.a.cent. (in touch with 61st Division).

    Main Line of Resistance - R.22.a.1.7.   to cross roads R.7.a.   (A map shewing the line will be issued).

3. The forward Brigades will maintain close touch with the enemy by means of patrols.   Should the enemy retire he will be at once followed up, but an organised attack will not be undertaken without orders from Divisional Headquarters.   (Separate instructions are being issued to Brigadiers).

4. The Field Artillery covering the front is divided into two Groups and consists of the following :-

    Right Group - Lieut-Col. MUSGRAVE, Headquarters RUESNES
                   3rd Div. Arty.   CHATEAU R.14.c.6.1.

    Left Group   - Lieut-Col. BARTON, Headquarters CAPELLE,
                   41st Bde. R.F.A.   Q.35.a.7.5.
                   14th Bde. R.H.A.

76th Bde. and 36th Bde. R.F.A. remain under the C.R.A. 2nd Division.

The Heavy Artillery available is as follows :-

84th Bde. R.G.A. - Lieut-Col. HEPPER, 2 6" How. and 2 60pdr. Batteries, affiliated to 2nd Division Headquarters D.5.b.9.2.

P.T.O.

- (2) -

    60th Bde. R.G.A. - Lieut-Col. NIVEN, 3 6" How. Batteries, affiliated to Right Inf. Brigade, Headquarters W.5.b.5.3.

    63rd Bde. R.G.A. - Lieut-Col. GRAY, 2 6" How. Batteries and 2 60pdr. Batteries, affiliated to Left Inf. Brigade, Headquarters Q.35.a.5.9.

5.   The disposition of Machine Guns is approximately

    1 Coy. each Brigade Section
    1 Coy. in Support positions
    1 Coy. in Reserve.

6.   Orders regarding the disposition of the Corps Mounted Troops will be issued later.

7.   Moves of Infantry Brigades are as follows (orders have been already issued).

    99th Inf. Brigade from SOLESMES to ESCARMAIN, in relief of 9th Inf. Brigade (to leave SOLESMES at 1000).

    6th Inf. Brigade to relieve 8th Inf. Brigade in Forward Area (Right). Not to pass VERTAIN before 1400.

    5th Inf. Brigade to relieve 76th Inf. Brigade in Forward Area (Left). Not to leave VERTAIN before 1530.

8.   Command of the Artillery covering the front will pass to C.R.A. 2nd Division at 1800, 29th October.

9.   Details of relief of Machine Guns will be arranged between Machine Gun Battalion Commanders. Command of the Machine Guns to pass to 2nd Machine Gun Battalion on completion of Infantry reliefs.

10 ....

- (3) -

10. Relief of Medical Units to be arranged between A.Ds.M.S.

11. Inter-Brigade boundaries will be :-

BOQUET de QUATORZE - Road junction R.20.a.2.8. - Road junction R.14.c.4.4. - Road junction R.14.b.2.1. (all inclusive to Right Brigade) - HALT R.9.c.0.7. - R.9.b.3.5. - MILL at VILLERS POL R.4.b.8.3. (last three inclusive to Left Brigade).

12. Orders for the move of Train Companies and S.A.A. Section are being issued by 2nd Division "Q".

13. Field Companies R.E. and 10th D.C.L.I. (Pioneers) will not move at present, and will continue working under the C.R.E.

14. Divisional Headquarters will remain at ST. PYTHON.

15. Command of the Divisional Advanced Guard will pass to G.O.C. 2nd Division on completion of Infantry reliefs.

16. ACKNOWLEDGE.

E R Clayton
Lieut-Colonel,
General Staff, 2nd Division.

Issued at 1050 to :-

Copy No.				
1	to	5th Inf. Brigade	11	61st Division
2		6th Inf. Brigade	12	New Zealand Division
3		99th Inf. Brigade	13	VI Corps
4		No. 2 M.G. Battn.	14	"Q" 2nd Division
5		C.R.A.	15	A.D.M.S.
6		C.R.E.	16	D.A.P.M.
7		2nd Signal Co.	17	Oxfordshire Hussars
8		10th D.C.L.I.	18	6th Cyclist Battn.
9		Guards Division	19 - 23	G.S. Records.
10		3rd Division		

2nd Division No. GR.4/2

5th Inf. Bde.
6th Inf. Bde.
99th Inf. Bde.

With reference to 2nd Division Order No.367 dated 29/10/18.

Herewith map shewing dispositions as given by the 3rd Division.

29/10/18

R C Firebrace
Major
For Lieut-Colonel
General Staff - 2nd Division

APPENDIX ~~XCVIII~~ a

SECRET.

2nd Division No. G.R. 4/3.

```
5th Inf. Brigade      M.G. Battn.
6th Inf. Brigade      2nd Signal Co.
99th Inf. Brigade     A.D.M.S.
C.R.A.                "Q"
C.R.E.
```

Instructions referred to in para. 3, 2nd Div. Order 367.

1. It is possible that the enemy may withdraw as he has previously done before dawn for a distance of 7 or 8 miles.

2. In order to find out at once if he withdraws and to be prepared to follow him up without delay, Brigades in the line will patrol vigorously. It is particularly necessary that touch with the enemy should be obtained just before dawn, A report giving the information obtained by patrols during the night (situation unchanged or otherwise) will reach Div. Headquarters by 0700 daily, in addition to the ordinary situation reports.

3. Brigadiers will ensure that Support and Reserve Battalions are ready to move forward without delay should the enemy withdraw. Corps Mounted Troops consisting 1 Company VI Corps Cyclists at present (at RUESNES R.14.d.8.3.) and 1 Troop of Oxfordshire Hussars (at ESCARMAIN) are at the disposal of the Division.

   These Troops are placed under the G.O.C. 6th Inf. Brigade who will use them for keeping touch with the enemy in the event of a withdrawal.

   The remainder of the Corps Cavalry Regt. is at BOUSSIERES and may possibly be made available later.

4. The C.R.A. will detail 2 Brigades R.F.A. to be ready to move forward with the 5th and 6th Inf. Brigades. The Os.C. Brigades R.F.A. will get in touch with Infantry Brigadiers at once.

5. One Machine Gun Coy. will be detailed to move forward with each of the 5th and 6th Inf. Brigades. The Company Commanders will get in touch with the Infantry Brigadiers.

6. The 99th Inf. Brigade will be prepared to support the advance of the 5th and 6th Inf. Brigades, and will be at one hour's notice to move from 0700 to 0900 daily.

7. Should an advance take place the C.R.E. will arrange that the detachment of Tunnellers now with the Division is ready to move forward, to search for and remove booby traps.

8. ACKNOWLEDGE.

E R Clayton
Lieut-Colonel,
General Staff, 2nd Division.

29th October, 1918.

SECRET.

2nd Division No. G.R. 4/3.

5th Inf. Brigade   M.G. Battalion
6th Inf. Brigade   2nd Signal Co.
99th Inf. Brigade   A.D.M.S.
C.R.A.   "Q"
C.R.E.

Instructions referred to in para. 3, 2nd Division Order 367.

1. It is possible that the enemy may withdraw as he has previously done before dawn for a distance of 7 or 8 miles.

2. In order to find out at once if he withdraws and to be prepared to follow him up without delay, Brigades in the line will patrol vigorously. It is particularly necessary that touch with the enemy should be obtained just before dawn; a report giving the information obtained by patrols during the night (situation unchanged or otherwise) will reach Div. Headquarters by 0700 daily, in addition to the ordinary situation reports.

3. Brigadiers will ensure that Support and Reserve Battalions are ready to move forward without delay should the enemy withdraw. Corps Mounted Troops consisting of 1 Company VI Corps Cyclists at present (at RUESNES R.14.d.5.3) and 1 Troop of Oxfordshire Hussars (at ESCARMAIN) are at the disposal of the Division.
     These Troops are placed under the G.O.C. 6th Infantry Brigade who will use them for keeping touch with the enemy in the event of a withdrawal.
     The remainder of the Corps Cavalry Regt. is at BOUSSIERES and may possibly be made available later.

4. The C.R.A. will detail 2 Brigades R.F.A. to be ready to move forward with the 5th and 6th Inf. Brigades. The Os.C. Brigades R.F.A. will get in touch with Infantry Brigadiers at once.

5. One Machine Gun Coy. will be detailed to move forward with each of the 5th and 6th Inf. Brigades. The Company Commanders will get in touch with the Infantry Brigadiers.

6. The 99th Inf. Brigade will be prepared to support the advance of the 5th and 6th Inf. Brigades, and will be at one hour's notice to move from 0700 tp 0900 daily.

7. Should an advance take place the C.R.E. will arrange that the detachment of Tunnellers now with the Division is ready to move forward, to search for and remove booby traps.

8. ACKNOWLEDGE.

(sgd) E.R. Clayton
Lieut-Colonel,
General Staff, 2nd Division.

29th October 1918.

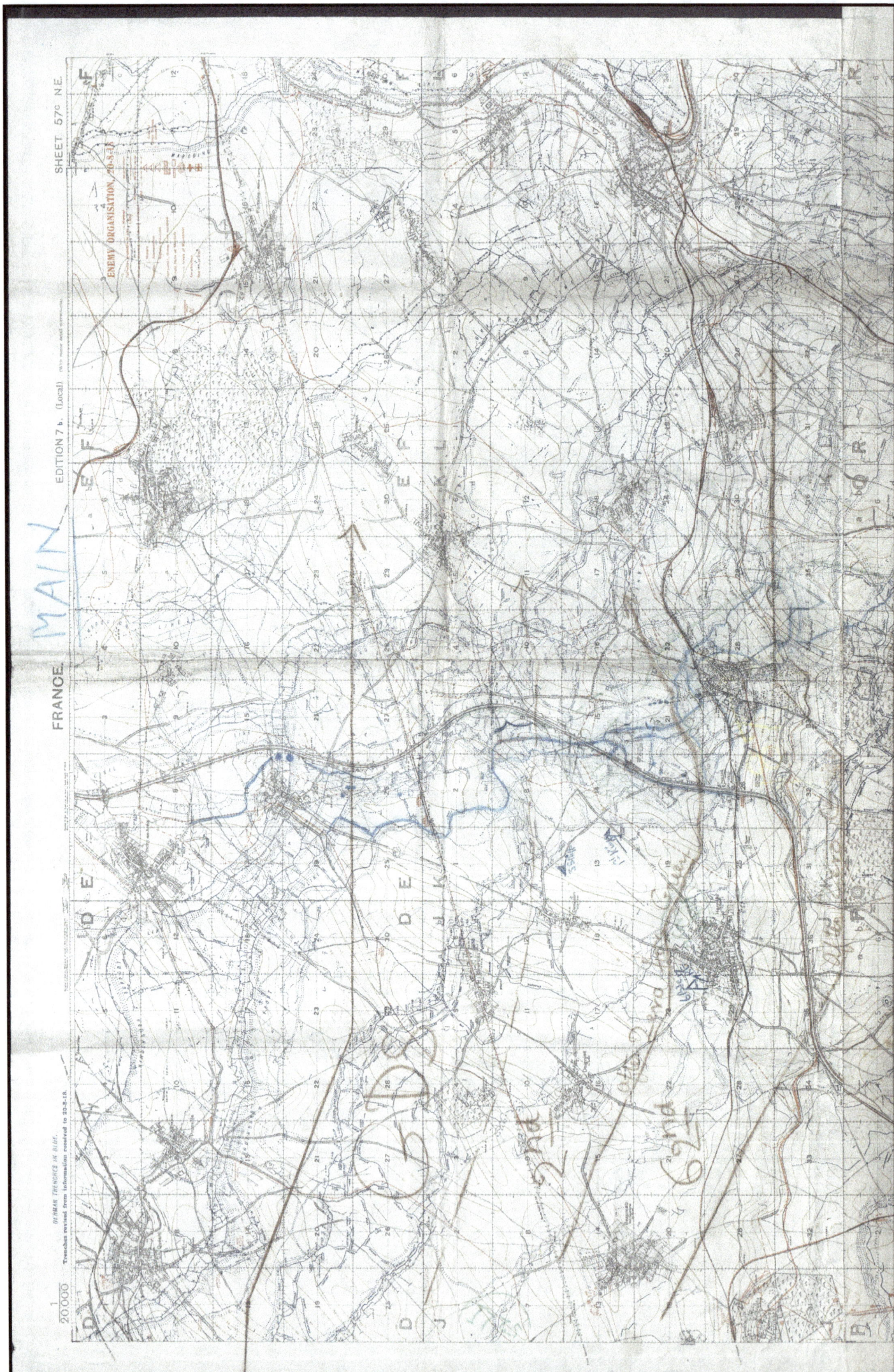

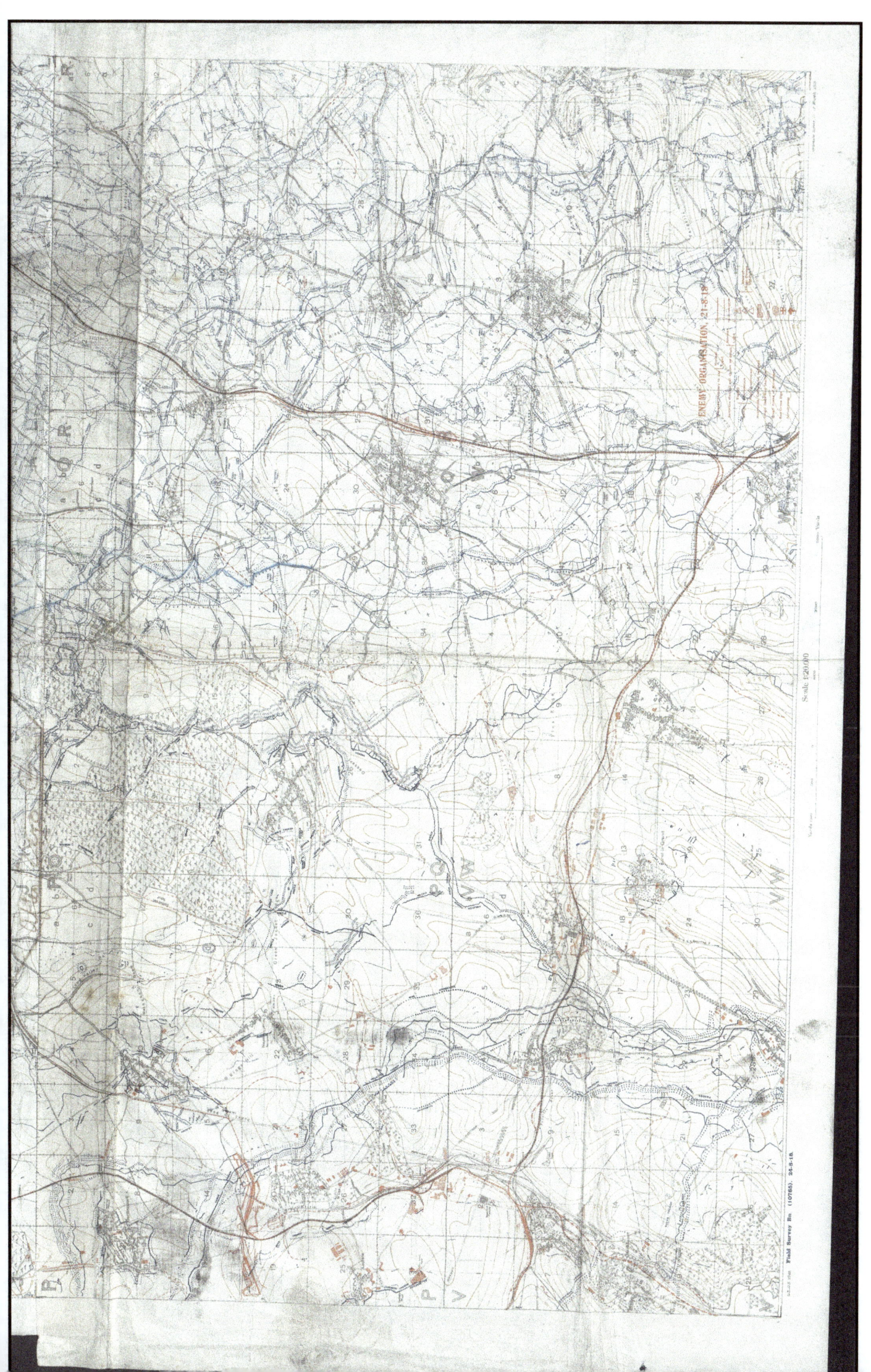

MAIN

Report on operations from 27th September.

2nd Signal Co. R.E.

27th September.

The forward party which was to lay the line shown in Red on attached map started out from DEMICOURT at 8.0 a.m. The work progressed quickly and after dropping a Relay post and lineman's post in the canal bank the line was laid up to SALLEY ALLEY. The 6th and 99th Brigades moved forward and were using the line and so kept in touch with Division.. A second Relay post and lineman's post was established in SALLEY ALLEY and a visual station was set up which worked back to DEMICOURT. At 2.30 p.m. the line was carried forward towards FLESQUIERES, the 6th and 99th Brigades continuing to use the line when they moved up to K.17.b.4.6. At this point they also picked up the line laid by the Guard's Divn., which gave an alternative means of communication back. The line was then taken forward almost to the Sugar Factory N.E. of FLESQUIERES.

During the course of the operations this line was most useful as it was from time to time as far forward as the attacking battalions. By this means much useful information was sent back by the forward party. It was not without difficulties that this line was laid as the party, on several occasions, were subjected to heavy shell fire and machine-gun fire which greatly hindered the work. The trouble taken however amply repaid itself as the line was seldom broken and the Brigades, by moving forward along the line, were kept in touch with the Division.

28th September.

At 4.0 a.m. the line was taken forward along the FLESQUIERES - MARCOING road for about one mile where it was then branched Northwards to the N.W. corner of NINE WOOD. Later in the morning the line was taken forward to NOYELLES.

At 2.30 p.m. Advanced Divn opened at L.13.c.1.3 and the Brigades moved forward, the 6th and 99th Brigades being in NOYELLES Prior to this the line proved to be of great value as it was used by the battalions who sent back much useful information regarding the bridges etc.

Visual.

After the 27th visual was not used owing ~~the~~ to the nature of the surroundings which were not favourable.

Wireless.

Wireless stations moved forward with the advancing troops and touch was always maintained. Few messages were sent by this means however as the communications by wire worked well.

Pigeons.

Were not used extensively but when used again proved their worth. The average time taken between front line and the Division was 2 hours.

Appendix. LESSONS LEARNT.

During these operations it was found to be absolutely essential to have lateral communication between Divisions.

Major.
Commanding 2nd Signal Co. R.E.

APPENDIX CIV

SECRET.

LOCATIONS 2ND DIVISION.

1st November 1918.

Reference Sheet 57b and 51a.   1/40,000.

2nd Division H.Q.	ST PYTHON. D.6.a.7.2.
2nd Signal Coy.	ST PYTHON.
C.R.A.	ST PYTHON. D.6.a.8.0.
36th Bde. R.F.A.)	Line.
41st Bde. R.F.A.)	
C.R.E.	D.6.a.5.7.
5th Field Coy. R.E.	Q.29.c.3.1.
226th Field Coy. R.E.	FERME de RIEUX. W.2.b.
483rd Field Coy. R.E.	W.2.b.7.9.
5th Infantry Brigade.	CAPELLE. Q.35.a.6.7. Rr.H.Q. W.15.d.3.8.
2nd Oxf. & Bucks L.I.	R.13.d.8.3.
2nd H.L.I.	Q.29.c.4.0.
24th R. Fusiliers.	R.14.c.1.4.
5th T.M. Battery.	Q.35.a.7.8.
6th Infantry Brigade.	RUESNES. R.20.b.1.6. Rr.H.Q. W.15.d.3.8.
1st Kings. Regt.	R.25.c.4.6.
2nd S. Staffs. Regt.	RUESNES. R.14.d.7.1.
17th R. Fusiliers.	R.14.b.3.3.
6th T.M. Battery.	R.25.c.0.7.
99th Infantry Brigade.	ESCARMAIN. W.5.d.1.6.
1st R. Berks. Regt.	W.5.a.5.1.
1st K.R.R.C.	W.4.d.85.75.
23rd R. Fusiliers.	W.5.c.05.55.
99th T.M. Battery.	W.5.d.2.8.
M.G. Battalion.	W.7.d.55.15.
"A" Company.	ESCARMAIN
"B" "	CAPELLE
"C" "	ESCARMAIN
"D" "	R.14.d.0.4.
10th D.C.L.I. (Pioneers)	W.9.d.8.9.
2nd Div. Reop. Camp.	BOUSSIERES. Haupt St. Billet No.14a.
Railhead Reop. Camp.	CAMBRAI ANNEXE STATION.
D.A.D.O.S.	ST. PYTHON
D.A.P.M.	ST. PYTHON
P. of W. Cage	CAPELLE
2nd Div. Train H.Q.	ST. PYTHON
S.A.A. Section H.Q.	V.30.b.6.0.

P.T.O.

A.D.M.S.	D.6.a.6.4.
Main Dressing Station.	ESCARMAIN
Adv. Dressing Station.	RUESNES. R.14.c.6.5.
5th Field Ambulance.	ESCARMAIN.
6th Field Ambulance.	ESCARMAIN. W.4.d.9.7.
100th Field Ambulance.	W.15.a.9.8.
Motor Ambulance Car Stand.	BREWERY, CAPELLE.
84th Bde. R.G.A.	W.5.a.9.3.
VI Corps H.Q.	GRAND CHANTEMEL.
Corps P. of W. Cage.	SOLESMES. (Hotel de Ville).
Mob Vet. Section.	ST HILAIRE. Billet No.12.
Vet. Aid Post.	W.15.b.1.1.
3rd Division.	QUIEVY.
62nd Division.	SOLESMES.
1 Troops Oxford Hussars.	W.4.d.9.6.
New Zealand Division.	SOLESMES. E.1.c.8.2.
1st N.Z. Brigade.	SOLESMES. E.1.d.1.2.
2nd N.Z. Brigade.	VERTIGNEUL. W.29.a.4.3.
3rd N.Z. Brigade.	X.2.a.6.5.
Guards Division.	BOUSSIERES.
1st Guards Brigade.	ST HILAIRE.
2nd Guards Brigade.	VERTAIN.
3rd Guards Brigade.	C.12.b.3.6.
61st Division.	VENDEGIES. Q.14.d.1.7.
182nd Infantry Brigade.	Q.4.c.6.7.
183rd Infantry Brigade.	LARBLIN. Q.16.a.
184th Infantry Brigade.	BERMERAIN. Q.22.a.5.2.

B. N. Haughton

Captain for
Lieut. Colonel.
General Staff. 2nd Division

APPENDIX CIII

SECRET

Copy No. 18

2nd DIVISION WARNING ORDER No. 368.   October 31st 1918.

1. The 2nd Division will be relieved in the line on November 2nd/3rd by the Guards Division on the left, and the 62nd Division on the right.

2. The boundary between the Guards Division and 62nd Division will be :-

   R.19.c.5.0. - Cross Roads R.14.c.3.3. - HALT R.9.c. (inclusive to Right Division) - LA CROISSETTE (inclusive to Left Division) - R.4.d.9.9.

3. After relief the 6th Brigade probably will be accommodated for the night November 2nd/3rd -

   2 Battalions ESCARMAIN
   1 Battalion ROMERIES

   5th Brigade -

   2 Battalions ESCARMAIN
   1 Battalion VERTAIN

   99th Brigade will probably move on November 2nd/3rd to ST. HILAIRE.

   Further moves will take place on November 3rd.

   There will be no movement of troops before 1630.

4. The machine guns will be relieved on November 2nd/3rd. The 2nd Machine Gun Battalion after relief will be concentrated at SOLESMES.

E R Clayton
Lieut-Colonel,
General Staff, 2nd Division.

Distribution overleaf.

Distribution:-

Copy No. 1	to	5th Inf. Brigade
2		6th Inf. Brigade
3		99th Inf. Brigade
4		No. 2 M.G. Battalion
5		C.R.A.
6		C.R.E.
7		2nd Signal Co.
8		10th D.C.L.I.
9		2nd Div. Train
10		Guards Division
11		61st Division
12		62nd Division
13		New Zealand Division
14		"Q" 2nd Division
15		A.D.M.S.
16 - 20		G.S. Records.

APPENDIX CII

SECRET.
2nd Division No. G.R. 4/9.

```
5th Inf. Bde.      C.R.E.
6th Inf. Bde.      Signals.
99th Inf. Bde.     10th D.C.L.I.
M.G. Battn.        "Q"
C.R.A.             A.D.M.S.
```

1. The Corps forward boundary has now been changed to :-

   <u>Northern Boundary.</u> from L.27.d.5.0. due East along the grid line at the bottom of squares L.28, L.29, etc.

   <u>Southern Boundary.</u> from R.16.d.0.0. due East along grid line at the bottom of squares R.17, R.18, etc.

2. ACKNOWLEDGE.

E R Clayton
Lieut. Colonel.
31st October 1918.   General Staff. 2nd Division.

APPENDIX CI

SECRET.

LOCATIONS 2ND DIVISION.   31st October. 1918.

Reference Sheet 57b and 51a.   1/40,000.

2nd Division H.Q.	ST PYTHON.	D.6.a.7.2.
2nd Signal Coy.	ST PYTHON.	
C.R.A.	ST PYTHON.	D.6.a.8.0.
36th Bde. R.F.A.)	Line.	
41st Bde. R.F.A.)		
C.R.E.	D.6.a.5.7.	
5th Field Coy. R.E.	Q.29.c.3.1.	
226th Field Coy. R.E.	W.15.b.8.8.	
83rd Field Coy. R.E.	W.2.b.7.9.	
5th Infantry Brigade.	CAPELLE. Q.35.a.6.7.	Rr. H.Q.W.15.d.3.8.
2nd Oxf. & Bucks L.I.	R.13.d.8.3.	
2nd H.L.I.	Q.29.c.4.0.	
24th R. Fusiliers.	R.14.c.1.4.	
5th T.M. Battery.	Q.35.a.7.8.	
6th Infantry Brigade.	RUESNES. R.20.b.1.6.	Rr H.Q.W.15.d.3.8.
1st Kings Regt.	R.25.c.4.6.	
2nd S. Staffs. Regt.	RUESNES. R.14.d.7.1.	
17th R. Fusiliers.	R.14.b.3.3.	
6th T.M. Battery.	R.25.c.0.7.	
99th Infantry Brigade.	ESCARMAIN. W.5.d.1.6.	
1st R. Berks. Regt.	W.5.a.5.1.	
1st K.R.R.C.	W.4.d.85.75.	
23rd R. Fusiliers.	W.5.c.05.55.	
99th T.M. Battery.	W.5.d.2.8.	
M.G. Battalion.	VERTAIN. W.15.a.9.3.	
"A" Company.	ESCARMAIN.	
"B" "	CAPELLE.	
"C" "	ESCARMAIN.	
"D" "	R.14.d.0.4.	
10th D.C.L.I. (Pioneers)	W.15.a.8.4.	
2nd Div. Recp. Camp.	BOUSSIERES. Haupt St. Billet No.14a.	
Railhead Recp. Camp.	CAMBRAI ANNEXE STATION.	
D.A.D.O.S.	ST PYTHON.	
D.A.P.M.	ST PYTHON.	
2nd Div. Train H.Q.	ST PYTHON.	
S.A.A. Section H.Q.	V.30.b.6.0.	

P.T.O.

- 2 -

A.D.M.S.	D.6.a.6.4.
Main Dressing Station.	ESCARMAIN.
Adv. Dressing Station.	RUESNES. R.14.c.6.5.
5th Field Ambulance.	ESCARMAIN.
6th Field Ambulance.	VERTAIN.
100th Field Ambulance.	ST PYTHON.
Motor Ambulance. Car Stand.	BREWERY, CAPELLE.
24th Bde. R.G.A.	D.5.b.90.25.
VI Corps H.Q.	GRAND CHANTEMEL.
Corps P. of W. Cage.	SOLESMES. (Hotel de Ville.)
Mob. Vet. Section.	ST HILAIRE. Billet No.12.
Vet. Aid Post.	W.15.b.1.1.
Guards Division.	BOUSSIERES.
62nd Division.	BEVILLERS.
1 Troop Oxford Hussars.	W.4.d.9.6.
New Zealand Division.	SOLESMES. E.1.c.8.2.
1st N.Z. Brigade.	SOLESMES. E.1.d.1.2.
2nd N.Z. Brigade.	VERTIGNEUL. W.29.a.4.3.
3rd N.Z. Brigade.	X.2.a.6.5.
3rd Division.	SOLESMES. E.1.c.6.8.
8th Infantry Brigade.	VERTAIN.
9th Infantry Brigade.	SOLESMES.
76th Infantry Brigade.	VERTAIN.
61st Division.	VENDEGIES. Q.14.d.1.7.
182nd Infantry Brigade.	VENDEGIES. Q.8.d.8.7.
183rd Infantry Brigade.	LARBLIN. Q.16.a.
184th Infantry Brigade.	BERMERAIN. Q.22.a.5.2.

R. N. Harrison
Captain for,
Lieut. Colonel.,
General Staff. 2nd Division.

APPENDIX C

S E C R E T.

2nd Division No. G.R. 4/7.

```
5th Inf. Brigade      10th D.C.L.I.
6th Inf. Brigade      2nd Signal Co.
99th Inf. Brigade     A.D.M.S.
C.R.A.                New Zealand Division
C.R.E.                61st Division
No. 2 M.G. Battn.
```

SECRET

In continuation of 2nd Division No. G.R. 4/3, dated 29th October.

1. In the event of an enemy attack there will be no retirement from the present outpost line.

2. The two Brigades in the Forward Area will be responsible for the defence as far back as the main line of resistance.

3. The Reserve Brigade will be ready to counter-attack or to reinforce the main line of resistance.

4. At present the Brigades in the line will carry on work on the main line of resistance.

5. The Machine Gun defence is organised with one Company in the Forward Area of each Brigade and one Company in support on the whole front. One Company is held in Reserve.

6. The main line of resistance is to be kept garrisoned. Should troops be moved forward from the main line of resistance for counter-attack or to reinforce they will be at once replaced from the Reserve Brigade.

7. Artillery barrages will be arranged to cover our present front line, and the main line of resistance, but no barrage will be put down to cover the main line of resistance without orders from Divisional Headquarters.

P.T.O.

- 2 -

8. The Corps Forward boundaries are as follows (already given in 2nd Division No. G. 80, dated 25th October) :-

   Right Boundary.

   R.22.a.0.0. - R.11.central - M.1.b.central - G.32.central - G.11.central - R.25.central.

   Left Boundary.

   R.7.a.7.2. - L.32.d.0.0. - L.28.a.0.0. - L.17.b.5.3. - L.12.c.0.0. - G.2.central - A.17.a.3.0. - A.12.central.

9. ACKNOWLEDGE.

E R Clayton
Lieut-Colonel,
General Staff, 2nd Division.

30th October, 1918.

APPENDIX XCIX

SECRET

LOCATIONS 2ND DIVISION.   30th October, 1918.

Reference Sheet 57b & 51a.   1/40,000.

2nd Division H.Q.	ST PYTHON.	D.6.a.7.2.
2nd Signal Coy.	ST PYTHON.	
C.R.A.	ST PYTHON.	D.6.a.8.0.
36th Bde. R.F.A.)		
41st Bde. R.F.A.)	Line.	
C.R.E.	D.6.a.5.7.	
5th Field Coy. R.E.	Q.29.c.3.1.	
226th Field Coy. R.E.	W.15.b.8.8.	
483rd Field Coy. R.E.	W.2.b.7.9.	
5th Infantry Brigade.	CAPELLE.	Q.35.a.6.7.
2nd Oxf. & Bucks L.I.)		
2nd H.L.I.)		
24th R. Fusiliers.)	Line. Loft.	
5th T.M. Battery.)		
6th Infantry Brigade.	RUESNES.	R.20.b.1.6.
1st Kings. Regt.	R.25. central.	
2nd S. Staffs. Regt.	RUESNES.	R.14.d.7.1.
17th R. Fusiliers.	RUESNES.	R.14.d.5.2.
6th T.M. Battery.	R.25.a.7.0.	
99th Infantry Brigade.	ESCARMAIN.	W.5.d.1.6.
1st R. Berks. Regt.	W.5.a.5.5.	
1st K.R.R.C.	W.4.d.85.75.	
23rd R. Fusiliers.	W.5.c.05.55.	
99th T.M. Battery.	W.5.d.2.8.	
M.G. Battalion.	VERTAIN.	W.15.a.9.3.
"A" Company.	ESCARMAIN.	
"B" "	CAPELLE.	
"C" "	ESCARMAIN.	
"D" "	R.20. central.	
10th D.C.L.I.(Pioneers)	W.15.a.8.4.	
2nd Div. Recp. Camp.	BOUSSIERES, Haupt St. Billot No.14a.	
Railhead Recp. Camp.	CAMBRAI ANNEXE Station.	
D.A.D.O.S.	ST PYTHON.	
D.A.P.M.	ST PYTHON.	
2nd Div. Train H.Q.	ST PYTHON.	
S.A.A. Section H.Q.	V.30.b.6.0.	

P.T.O.

- 2 -

A.D.M.S.	D.6.a.6.4.
Main Dressing Station.	ESCARMAIN.
Adv. Dressing Station.	RUESMES. R.14.c.6.5.
5th Field Ambulance.	ESCARMAIN.
6th Field Ambulance.	VERTAIN.
100th Field Ambulance.	ST PYTHON.
Motor Ambulance. Car Stand.	BREWERY, CAPELLE.
84th Bde. R.G.A.	D.5.b.90.25.
VI Corps H.Q.	GRAND CHANTEMEL.
Corps P. of W. Cage.	SOLESMES. (Hotel de Ville).
Guards Division.	BOUSSIERES.
62nd Division.	BEVILLERS.
New Zealand Division.	SOLESMES.
3rd N.Z. Brigade.	X.2.a.6.5.
1 Troop Oxford Hussars.	W.4.d.9.6.
3rd Division.	SOLESMES. E.1.c.8.8.
8th Infantry Brigade.	VERTAIN.
9th Infantry Brigade.	SOLESMES.
76th Infantry Brigade.	VERTAIN.
61st Division.	VENDEGIES. Q.14.d.1.7.
182nd Infantry Brigade.	VENDEGIES. Q.8.d.8.7.
183rd Infantry Brigade.	LAPELIN. Q.16.a.
184th Infantry Brigade.	BERMERAIN. Q.22.a.5.2.

B. N. Harrison

Captain for,
Lieut. Colonel.,
General Staff. 2nd Divn.

2nd Division No. G.S.1749.

5th Inf. Bde.
6th Inf. Bde.
99th Inf. Bde.
C.R.A.
C.R.E.
2/M.G.Battn.
10/D.C.L.I.
A.D.M.S.
2/Signal Coy.

---

1. Please forward a report on operations from 27th September as soon as you conveniently can.

2. Maps illustrating the various phases of your report would be a great assistance.

3. In addition to the formal report which has to be rendered by the Division, a narrative in more popular form is being prepared, and any information or reports from units which would be of value in this connection would be welcome and would be returned when done with if desired.

4. Any lessons or points which you wish to bring forward should be submitted as an appendix.

4/10/18.

Lieut.Colonel,
General Staff, 2nd Division.

CHANGES IN NOMINAL ROLLS OF OFFICERS (Cont'd)

Unit.	Joined.	Struck off.	Cause.
99th INFANTRY BRIGADE.			
23rd Royal Fusiliers.			
2/Lt. T.A. HUTCHINSON.	7-10-18.		Reinforcement.
2/Lt. J. FAIR.	7-10-18.		Do.
2/Lt. G.F. JAMES.	9-10-18.		Do.
2/Lt. F.B. WELLS.		10-10-18.	Died of wounds 10-10-18.
2/Lt. J.H. COWELL.		8-10-18.	Wounded 8-10-18.
1st Royal Berks Regt.			
Lt. E.L. JERWOOD, M.C.	}		
2/Lt. H.E.HALE.	} 8-10-18.		Reinforcements.
Lt. G. LAPWORTH.	}		
3 Officers.			Reinforcements. (Advised as leaving Base but not yet joined).
Lt. C.C. HEDGES, M.C.		8-10-18.	Missing.
2/Lt. L.E. SAVILLE.		8-10-18.	Do.
2/Lt. W. TOBEY.			
2/Lt. G.H. BARKER.		8-10-18.	Wounded.
2/Lt. K.B. GANDYPOLE.			
2/Lt. W. MURRAY.		30-9-18.	To England sick 26-9-18. (Auth: D.A.G.List No. 1288 dated 30-9-18)
1st K.R.Rifle Corps.			
Lt. H.G. SCHAEFFER.	}		
2/Lt. A.W. SCHAEFFER.	} 6-10-18.		Reinforcements.
2/Lt. H.T. FICE.	}		
2/Lt. G.H. CAMPBELL.	} 7-10-18.		Reinforcements.
2/Lt. T.G. WELSH.	}		
2/Lt. M.W. BIRD.		8-10-18.	Wounded.
2/Lt. R.J. ANDREWS.		8-10-18.	Do.
10th D.C.L.I.			
Capt. C.B. JENRICK.		5-10-18.	To England sick 30-9-18. (Auth: D.A.G.List No. 1276 dated 5-10-18).
No.2 Bn. M.G.Corps.			
Lt. J.B. NOLAN.	} 7-10-18.		Reinforcements.
2/Lt. A.V. FRANKLIN.	}		
Lt. R.B. PRICE.	} 10-10-18.		Do.
Lt. R.M. KIMBALL, M.C.	}		
Lt. E.S. RAMON, M.C.		7-10-18.	Evacuated sick.
Lt. E.G. MEADER.		7-10-18.	Do.
Lt. D.H. CORNELLES.		9-10-18.	To G.H.Q. M.G.School 9-10-18. (Auth: AG/GG/1548(c) dated 6-10-18.

REINFORCEMENTS OF OFFICERS AND MEN.
OTHER RANKS.

UNIT.	INCREASE.	DECREASE.

5th INFANTRY BRIGADE.

13th Royal Fusiliers. — 54 Reinforcements and Casuals. — 2 Killed. 10 Wounded. 16 Sick. 2 Other Causes.

2nd Oxf. & Bucks L.I. — 36 Reinforcements. — 2 Killed. 5 Wounded. 11 Evacuated sick.

2nd Highland L.I. — 11 Reinforcements. — 6 Battle casualties. 9 Evacuated sick. 1 Commission.

6th INFANTRY BRIGADE.

17th Royal Fusiliers. — 54 Reinforcements. 2 From hospital. 1 Miscellaneous. — 4 Killed. 7 Missing. 17 Wounded. 31 Evacuated sick.

1st King's Regiment. — 79 Reinforcements. 11 From hospital. — 18 Evacuated sick. 2 Killed. 9 Wounded. 1 Wounded and missing.

2nd S.Staffs Regt. — 71 Reinforcements. — 3 Killed. 38 Wounded. 1 Missing. 9 Evacuated sick. 1 Base Depot.

99th INFANTRY BRIGADE.

23rd Royal Fusiliers. — 67 Reinforcements & from hospital. — 67 Wounded. 12 Killed. 3 Wounded (Acc.S.I.) 9 Missing. 5 Evacuated sick.

1st Royal Berks Regt. — 29 Reinforcements & from hospital. — 86 Wounded. 17 Killed. 1 Wounded (S.I.) 4 D.V.D. 15 Evacuated sick. 12 Missing.

1st K.R.Rifle Corps. — 10 Reinforcements. 5 From hospital. — 30 Evacuated sick. 18 Killed. 9 Missing. 73 Wounded. 1 Base, undergo.

10th D.C.L.I. (Pioneers). — 4 From hospital. — 2 Wounded. 6 Evacuated sick.

No. 2 Bn. M.G.Corps. — 38 Reinforcements. 5 From hospital. — 10 Casualties. 8 Evacuated sick. 2 To U.K. for Special Course. 2 To Base Depot.

	K.	W.	M
99 Bde.	47	230	30
17 RF	4	17	7

EXPLANATION OF COLUMN "E".

(a) On leave.
(b) Sick.
(c) Attending Courses.
(d) Detailed for specific duties etc.
(e) Extra regimentally employed.

UNIT.		Off.	O.R.
8th INFANTRY BRIGADE.			
2nd Royal Fusiliers.	(a)	4	81
	(b)	-	12
	(c)	-	8
	(d)	-	-
	(e)	5	51
		9	152
2nd Oxf. & Bucks L.I.	(a)	3	81
	(b)	-	10
	(c)	1	7
	(d)	-	-
	(e)	3	69
		7	167
2nd Highland L.I.	(a)	1	55
	(b)	2	8
	(c)	-	11
	(d)	-	-
	(e)	1	41
		4	115
9th INFANTRY BRIGADE.			
17th Royal Fusiliers.	(a)	2	30
	(b)	3	15
	(c)	3	16
	(d)	-	2
	(e)	-	39
		8	102
1st King's Regiment.	(a)	3	47
	(b)	-	16
	(c)	3	10
	(d)	-	1
	(e)	2	23
		8	107
2nd S.Staffs Regt.	(a)	3	40
	(b)	6	5
	(c)	3	20
	(d)	1	3
	(e)	-	41
		13	109
99th INFANTRY BRIGADE.			
23rd Royal Fusiliers.	(a)	1	45
	(b)	2	10
	(c)	2	14
	(d)	-	2
	(e)	3	°44 ° 21 s O.R. advised but not yet joined.
		8	115
1st Royal Berks Regt.	(a)	1	55
	(b)	3	6
	(c)	3	16
	(d)	-	3
	(e)	-	°41 ° 2 O.R. Absentees.
		9	119

P.T.O.

99th INFANTRY BRIGADE. (Cont'd)   Off. O.R.
1st K.R.Rifle Corps. (a)   4   45
                      (b)   3   19
                      (c)   3   14
                      (d)   -   --
                      (e)   1   40
                           ---- ----
                            11   118

10th D.C.L.I. (Pioneers) (a) 4   41
                         (b) 1   11
                         (c) -   8
                         (d) -   --
                         (e) 1   15
                             ---- ----
                              6   75

No. 3 Bn., M.G.Corps. (a)   5   65
                       (b)   -   9
                       (c)   -   5
                       (d)   -   -
                       (e)   -   1
                           ---- ----
                             5   70

EXPLANATION OF INCREASE AND DECREASE.
OTHER RANKS.

UNIT.	INCREASE.	DECREASE.
5th INFANTRY BRIGADE.		
24th Royal Fusiliers.	15 From Hospital.	1 Wounded.
		8 Evacuated sick.
		4 Miscellaneous.
2nd Oxf. & Bucks L.I.	44 Reinforcements.	3 Wounded.
		10 Evacuated sick.
2nd Highland L.I.	212 Reinforcements.	2 Evacuated sick.
		1 Deserter.
6th INFANTRY BRIGADE.		
17th Royal Fusiliers.	16 Reinforcements.	1 Wounded (gas).
	1 Transfer.	15 Evacuated sick.
1st King's Regt.	11 From Hospital.	11 Evacuated sick.
	1 Transfer.	2 Commissions.
2nd S.Staffs Regt.	29 Reinforcements.	1 Wounded.
		1 Transferred to M.G.Corps.
		5 Base Depot.
99th INFANTRY BRIGADE.		
23rd Royal Fusiliers.	35 Reinforcements.	1 Commission.
		1 To Base, underage.
		8 Evacuated sick.
1st Royal Berks Regt.	36 Reinforcements.	1 Commission.
	13 From Hospital.	1 Transferred to 2nd R.Berks.
		3 Do. 99th T.M.B.
		2 Absentees.
		15 Evacuated sick.
1st K.R.Rifle Corps.	29 Reinforcements	4 Transferred to 99th T.M.B.
	and Casuals.	12 Evacuated sick.
		2 Commissions.
		4 To Base Depot.
		1 Transferred to 17th R.Fus.
10th D.C.L.I.(Pioneers)	2 Reinforcements.	17 Evacuated sick.
	5 From Hospital.	
No.2 Bn. M.G.Corps.	40 Reinforcements.	10 Evacuated sick.
	2 From Hospital.	
	1 Transferred from Infantry.	

EXPLANATION OF COLUMN "B".

(a) On leave.
(b) Sick.
(c) Attending Courses.
(d) Detailed for specific duties etc.
(e) Extra regimentally employed.

UNIT.		Off.	O.R.
5th INFANTRY BRIGADE.			
24th Royal Fusiliers.	(a)	5	82
	(b)	-	6
	(c)	1	6
	(d)	-	-
	(e)	4	53
		10	147
2nd Oxf. & Bucks L.I.	(a)	5	63
	(b)	-	8
	(c)	1	7
	(d)	-	-
	(e)	2	49
		8	127
2nd Highland L.I.	(a)	3	61
	(b)	2	7
	(c)	-	7
	(d)	-	-
	(e)	1	41
		6	116
6th INFANTRY BRIGADE.			
17th Royal Fusiliers.	(a)	3	51
	(b)	3	8
	(c)	3	12
	(d)	-	2
	(e)	-	37
		9	110
1st King's Regiment.	(a)	5	71
	(b)	-	8
	(c)	2	10
	(d)	-	1
	(e)	1	25
		8	115
2nd S.Staffs Regt.	(a)	6	53
	(b)	5	3
	(c)	2	21
	(d)	-	4
	(e)	1	40
		14	121
99th INFANTRY BRIGADE.			
23rd Royal Fusiliers.	(a)	2	66
	(b)	2	10
	(c)	2	11
	(d)	-	2
	(e)	3	39
		9	128
1st Royal Berks Regt.	(a)	2	39
	(b)	3	4
	(c)	4	15
	(d)	-	-
	(e)	* 3	38
		12	96

* 2 Officers not yet joined.

P.T.O.

		Off.	O.R.
9?th INFANTRY BRIGADE (Cont'd)			
1st K.R.Rifle Corps.	(a)	4	35
	(b)	2	20
	(c)	2	20
	(d)	-	2
	(e)	3	39
		11	116

10th D.C.L.I.(Pioneers)	(a)	6	34
	(b)	-	8
	(c)	-	10
	(d)	-	-
	(e)	1	6
		7	58

No.2 Bn. M.G.Corps.	(a)	6	64
	(b)	1	11
	(c)	-	5
	(d)	-	1
	(e)	-	-
		7	81

Map 3
Recovery Plans

SECRET

2nd Division No. GR.5/1

5th Inf. Bde.

With reference to 5th Bde. No.GS.740/252, para.3. Two Companies of the Support Battalion of 5th Bde. are 6,000 yards behind the front line; if, therefore, operations are suspended until the Support Battalion has passed through the Leading Battalion it will be approximately one and a half hours after the rear Companies of the Support Battalion move off before they can pass through the present front line.

The G.O.C. therefore considers that your Leading Battalion should be used for occupying the high ground to the N.E. of VILLERS-POL, the Support and Reserve Battalions being brought up to continue the advance.

30/10/18

E R Clayton
Lieut-Colonel
General Staff - 2nd Division

S E C R E T.

2nd Division No. G.R. 4/6.

G.O.C. 5th Inf. Brigade
G.O.C. 6th Inf. Brigade
G.O.C. 99th Inf. Brigade
O.C. No. 2 M.G. Battalion

The operations forecasted in 2nd Division No. G.R. 4/4, forwarded to you on October 29th are postponed for 24 hours.

30th Oct. 1918.

Lieut-Colonel,
General Staff, 2nd Division.

S E C R E T.

2nd Division No. G.R. 4/10.

5th Inf. Brigade
6th Inf. Brigade
99th Inf. Brigade
No. 2 M.G. Battalion
C.R.A.

With reference to 2nd Division No. G.R. 4/3, dated 29th October.

Should the enemy withdraw from the front now held by the Division (vide 2nd Division G.R. 4/9 - alteration of VI Corps Forward Boundary) he will be followed up in an Easterly direction.

The G.O.C. wishes special vigilance to be observed on the morning of November 2nd, as it is possible that after the attack of the XVII Corps and First Army on the morning of November 1st, the enemy may withdraw.

31st October, 1918.

E R Clayton
Lieut-Colonel,
General Staff, 2nd Division.

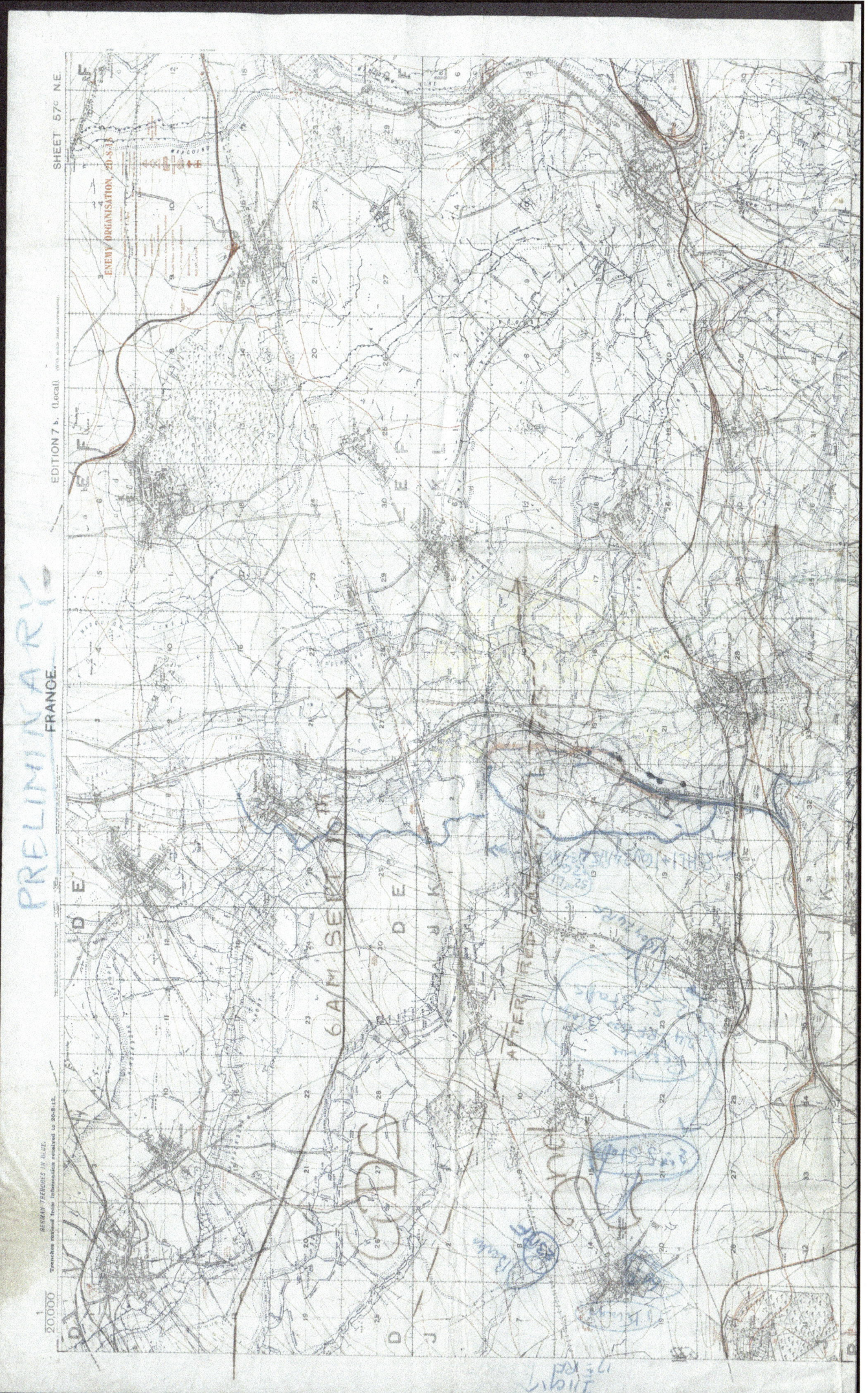

PRELIMINARY

www.ingramcontent.com/pod-product-compliance
Lightning Source LLC
Chambersburg PA
CBHW080849230426
43662CB00013B/2055